KU-257-831

THE SCIENCE CENTURY

Other books by Magnus Pyke

Nothing Like Science
Slaves Unaware?
The Science Myth
Food Science and Technology
The Manual of Nutrition (H.M.S.O.)
Industrial Nutrition (MACDONALD & EVANS)
Nutrition (E.U.P.)
The Boundaries of Science (HARRAP)

The
Science Century

MAGNUS PYKE

JOHN MURRAY
FIFTY ALBEMARLE STREET LONDON

To Bessie

SOUTHWARK COLLEGE FOR
FURTHER EDUCATION
THE CUT, LONDON, S.E.1

[609]

5250

© Magnus Pyke 1967

Printed in Great Britain
for John Murray
by Butler & Tanner Ltd,
Frome and London

CONTENTS

ILLUSTRATIONS

ACKNOWLEDGEMENTS

Grateful acknowledgement is given to the following for supplying original photographs for reproduction.

Aerofilms and Aero Pictorials Ltd—37
Associated Press Ltd—15
Boymans–van Beuningen Museum, Rotterdam—8
British Aircraft Corporation—22
British Transport Ltd—46
British Travel Association—24
Cassell & Co. Ltd. from W. Thornbury's *Old and New London*—34
Clarks Ltd—33
Deutsches Museum, Munich—9
Dornier Archiv-Photo—21
Farmer & Stockbreeder Publications Ltd—40, 41, 42
Ford Motor Co. Ltd—19
Greater London Council—20, 35
H.M. Postmaster-General—6, 25, 27
Illustrated London News—12, 13, 14
The International Wool Secretariat—30, 31
John Lobb & Co.—32
Massey-Ferguson Holdings Ltd—39
Mustograph Agency—38
Donald Paterson—43
Radio Times Hulton Picture Library—1, 2, 4, 7, 23, 26, 28, 36
Royal Holloway College—18
St Bartholomew's Hospital and Medical College—10
Science Museum—5
Brian Seed—11
Sunday Times—45
Transport Museum, Clapham—3
The Trustees of the Tate Gallery, London—17
United States Information Service—29
Westland Aircraft Ltd—16

CHAPTER I

A HUNDRED YEARS AGO

A hundred years is little more than the span of a man's lifetime. My mother, who died when I was fifty, was born in 1870; my grandmother, who died when I was twelve, was born in 1839, when Queen Victoria was a girl. How strange it now seems that these two people whose lives were tangled with my own lived most of their years in a world quite different from that of the present. The difference between Europe in the eighteenth century before the French Revolution and Europe afterwards was great, to be sure, yet the attitudes of the nineteenth-century men and women described by Tolstoy in *War and Peace*—when Napoleon, thrown up by the Revolution, was growing and growing as a force dominating the Western world—were much the same as those of Boswell's acquaintances of the eighteenth century or of the political society described a century earlier still by Pepys. The radical change that has since taken place in life and manners—this human revolution—is due to something quite new in history: applied science.

Mankind in the course of history has, as a thinking animal, produced a number of ideas. The idea of science, the notion that the universe and much of man's behaviour in it can be understood by precise observation followed by speculation, but speculation continuously submitted to experimental and observational verification (because this is what science is)—this intellectual invention has been one of the most explosive ideas of all. It is a philosophical idea yet, at the same time, it is the source of continuous technical innovation.

Science in its present form began in the heads of a handful of men in the seventeenth century: the members of the Royal Society of London, dominated by Sir Isaac Newton and a few other natural philosophers, as they then considered themselves, in France, Italy and the Low Countries. The numbers grew and in the eighteenth century the foundations of physics and chemistry were laid. Each decade the numbers doubled. The nineteenth century saw the great discoveries of Pasteur, Darwin and Mendel, the consolidation of

1

chemistry, the beginnings of the upsurge of technology. There is no reason to quarrel with Lord Bowden's calculation that of all the scientists who ever lived the majority are still alive today.

The pace at which science and technology have intruded into social life is clearly shown by the reports of the Great Exhibition of 1851 held in the Crystal Palace specially erected to contain it in Hyde Park in London. Today our life is cushioned at every point on 'plastics'; none of these was available in 1851. Modern industry and transport could hardly operate without rubber. In the enthusiastic account of the last word in science of 1851 we read of rubber:

> At the latter end of the last century and the beginning of the present it was brought into this country (Great Britain) in small quantities, where, on account of its being used for rubbing out black-lead pencil marks, it acquired the name of India-rubber. . . . While in England the employment of caoutchouc [rubber] was being developed principally in regard to the rendering of clothes waterproof [for which we are indebted to Messrs Mackintosh and Hancock] and in France its elasticity was being made available to the manufacture of certain tissues, it was turned to account in America for waterproofing shoes, by making use of the processes discovered by Mr Charles Goodyear.*

The social life of the twentieth century requires for its proper functioning light, power and communications. When we say, 'The lights have failed,' we mean that *electric* light has failed. A Cabinet minister, a business man, a lawyer, a journalist, even a family group— all these depend on the *electric* telephone. Our social fabric is supported by vacuum cleaners, polishers, washing machines and toasters —all using electricity—not by servants. Manufacture of every sort, motor-cars, aeroplanes, diesel-electric locomotives: all require electricity. Yet in 1851, electricity did not enter into the life of the citizen. Even when the contemporary commentator draws special attention to a 'telegraph' he is referring to something which, although it was a novelty in his time, is now forgotten. The account runs:

> The bell telegraph, otherwise called an 'annunciator', is an invention made to supersede the awkward array of bells in houses and hotels. It is an extremely neat and beautiful article, and indicates where the bell was rung by uncovering a number corresponding to the number of the room; and this, too, for any length of time afterwards, until, by the touch of a spring, the number is re-covered.†

* *The Great Exhibition of the World's Industry*, Tullis, London, 4 vols, 1851.
† Ibid.

In 1851 the great improvements in lighting were not the use of electricity but novel ideas for gas lamps and the introduction of paraffin, a petroleum product. Here again is what the writer of the time had to say:

> Marvellous are the uses . . . to which science has rendered heat subservient; these which have been obtained from light by the combinations of the researches of the mechanical philosopher have not been less striking. Ready-made flame is fabricated in vast establishments. . . .
> Lamps in which artificial light is produced by means of liquid combustible may be reduced to two classes; one in which the liquid is drawn to the wick by capillary attraction, and the other in which it is propelled by mechanic agency . . . by far the most brilliant in its illuminating power is one of recent introduction, called the camphine-lamp.*

One more example of what excited the people of 1851 demonstrates the difference between our world and that of a century ago: the thrill of the discovery of photography. Today, photography is a commonplace fact of life. It is used as routine for passports, in police records, catalogues, works of scholarship, newspapers, surveying and mapping, to study the surface of the moon, or to record the baby's first steps or the family holiday at the seaside. At the Great Exhibition, the daguerreotype—a picture recorded photographically on a copper plate—was a novelty. 'The discovery of the beautiful application of the chemical properties of light,' wrote the contemporary commentator, 'is of very recent date. . . .'

A hundred years ago the seeds of science were sown, but the plant—which like Jonah's gourd was to overshadow and change human life—had not yet grown up. Steam engines had been introduced into mines to keep them pumped free of water; steam power was used in factories; and Great Britain, the first country to enter the Industrial Revolution, was changing from an agricultural into a manufacturing nation; and railway lines were being built all over the land. Even so, the world over which the young Queen Victoria ruled was not very different from that of Queen Anne.

Science, as a way of thinking, is essentially a dynamic philosophy. The so-called 'laws of science' are quite different from legal pronouncements or the fixed doctrines of religion based on written scriptures. Scientific assertions are constantly under challenge. The Honourable

* Ibid.

3

Robert Boyle arranged a series of experiments in which the volume of a certain quantity of gas confined in a closed tube was subjected to increasing degrees of pressure. He found from this that when the pressure was doubled the volume of the gas was halved. From these experiments he deduced the general proposition that the volume of a gas, at any selected temperature, was inversely proportional to the pressure. This proposition is commonly called by British scientists, 'Boyle's Law'. Since 1685, when it was first propounded, it has served as a useful approximation in a number of practical situations, but at the same time it has been subjected to continual reappraisal. In fact, while it describes reasonably well what happens it is now known not to be precisely true. The same process of re-examination, of search for minimum inaccuracy, sometimes of discard of whole areas of accepted scientific belief, is an essential part of scientific thought. Newton's 'laws of motion' must stand trial with the rest and make way for the greater truth of Einstein; the phlogiston theory of combustion, firmly held by Joseph Priestley to the day of his death, must collapse in face of the new facts and better explanation of Lavoisier; even the 'law of conservation of matter', the cornerstone of chemical science for 200 years, must be rewritten to take into account the fresh facts of nuclear physics.

A hundred years or so ago it had not yet been realised that this way of thinking upon which science is based—the dynamic philosophy which insists that theories, 'laws', beliefs and assertions must be changed or abandoned altogether as soon as observations show them to be inadequate descriptions of reality—applies to everything. Indeed, this has not been fully understood today in spite of the weight of evidence that shows it to be inevitable. In an age when it was accepted that absolute wisdom was to be found in the writings of the ancients —the Books of Moses, the words of Aristotle on the pronouncement of legitimate kings—the essential stability of society was assured. But as soon as the observations and reasoning of Copernicus and Galileo were seen to imply that the earth is not the firm stable foundation of the universe round which everything else revolves but quite the contrary, then—when it is accepted that the earth is merely a minor satellite flying around a second-class star—the stability not only of the earth but also of the intellectual outlook of the men on it was destroyed. In its place came a dynamic, questioning philosophy: absolute truth—about the solar system and the system of social behaviour as well—is not, it seems, revealed in a supernatural flash; it must be painfully worked for by constant endeavour.

Even before Darwin and Wallace first published the evidence upon which the theory of evolution was based and before Darwin's *Origin of Species* came out—and became an immediate bestseller—intelligent people were already troubled in their minds, no matter how hard they tried to deny it to themselves, about the scriptural account of the Flood. As more and more animals were found to exist—giraffes, elephants, spiny ant-eaters, skunks—the notion that pairs of each of these could possibly have been housed in the ark built by Noah and his three sons to the quite precise specifications given in the Book of Genesis appeared more and more incredible. If people are prepared to follow the logic of the variations in animal species and the evidence of fossil forms recovered from rocks of the various geological periods, then they are brought inevitably to certain conclusions as to the truth of the situation. If this conclusion is different from that laid down by dogmatic authority, then a choice must be made, whether to accept the conclusions reached by the logic of scientific philosophy or not. And when it can be seen that new understanding of the origin of species, the law of gravity, or the nature of fire and combustion are reached by using the methods of science, it is tempting to apply the same methods to assess the effectiveness of, say, different methods of punishment, ways of feeding children, or even government itself. And since science is a process of constant doubting, re-verification and readjustment, it follows that it must produce the same element of doubt and uncertainty about such previously unchallenged matters as the perfect rectitude of the British Way of Life or the absolute veracity of the Book of Genesis.

Science makes itself manifest in two distinct ways. The first is the development of understanding about such matters as the nature of chemical combination or the mathematical principles governing the laws of gravity. The second is in the manner in which a community *uses* its scientific knowledge: whether it goes to work to make an efficient steam engine once the 'latent heat' of steam has been understood or uses the laws of electro-magnetism to construct a telephone. The time-lag between possessing the necessary scientific knowledge and using it is partly a matter of chance and partly a question of how much people want to apply the scientific knowledge they have to practical affairs. In the present modern age, new knowledge and new ideas based on new knowledge are applied very quickly. For example, each year we expect motor-cars to be an improvement on those available the year before. We expect glass-fibre to replace sheet steel, new substances to be developed to allow greasing to be put off until 3,000 miles have been run instead of a mere 1,000. New fabrics, new synthetic rubbers for the tyres, new anti-knock compounds in the petrol, improved brake-linings—all these applications of science are expected as the reward for research, and our expectations are not disappointed. The new discoveries are made and the old ones become obsolete.

Before the century of science began, people's outlook on affairs was different. The characters about whom Miss Jane Austen wrote in the first half of the nineteenth century travelled at a speed no faster than that of 3,000 years before: the speed of a horse. When Lady Catherine de Bergh came from her country seat to forbid Miss Elizabeth Bennett to marry her nephew Mr Darcy, she travelled, for all her wealth and pomp, in a horse-drawn carriage. When dashing young Mr Churchill went to London to have his hair cut, he rode on a horse, just as D'Artagnan in the fifteenth century and Absalom, who was so unfortunately caught by his hair while galloping under a tree, had done 1,500 years before.

Miss Emma Woodhouse is described as a strong-minded 'modern' young woman who admirably managed her father's housekeeping. Yet when she went to a dance the ballroom was illuminated by candles—of superfine quality to be sure but differing little from those used to light ballrooms in Queen Elizabeth's day, four centuries before. And the candle-makers had not even succeeded in solving so obvious and urgent a technical problem as how to prepare a wick that would not need to be snuffed. Today, we confidently expect electric lamp bulbs to be better than they were ten years ago, let alone four hundred, and we are not at all surprised when tungsten filaments supersede carbon filaments, gas-filled bulbs take the place of vacuum bulbs, and fluorescent lamps cause filament bulbs to disappear altogether. In spite of the signal advances in medicine which preceded Miss Austen's day—for example, William Harvey's discovery of the circulation of the blood in the seventeenth century and the introduction of vaccination by Jenner as a protection against smallpox in the eighteenth—much of the practice of medicine and the whole outlook of ordinary people to sickness and disease remained as it had been for ages. Mr Woodhouse when comparing the virtues of his physician, Mr Perry, with those of Mr Wingfield, the practitioner whose advice was obtained by his married daughter, could praise Mr Perry for recommending sea bathing at Cromer to strengthen the chest whereas Mr Wingfield put more faith in red flannel and the peculiarly bracing air of Southend.

'Highbury, the large and populous village, almost amounting to a town, to which Hartfield, in spite of its separate lawn, and shrubberies, and name, did really belong, afforded [Emma] no equals. The Woodhouses were first in consequence there. All looked up to them.' This was written between February 1811 and August 1816. Today, Highbury is a district of London, crowded in between Holloway, Finsbury Park, Stoke Newington and Islington. If young Mr Churchill wished to go into town to have his hair cut now, he would not need to take the whole day, nor would he ride into Central London on a horse. To start with, the animal would hardly be able to survive the traffic. Today, Mr Churchill would take a Moorgate electric train on the Underground and change at Old Street. Mr Woodhouse could no longer expect to be first in consequence nor could he drive in his carriage along the country road from his own house to dine with his neighbours, Mr and Mrs Weston. Today, his house would be numbered in a street and for twenty miles or more all round him would be town. Beyond him he would find more and more houses, in Tottenham, Walthamstow, Hornsey, Muswell Hill—mile after mile of unbroken houses and paved streets choked with traffic.

Poor, nervous Mr Woodhouse could no more survive in the Highbury of the second half of the twentieth century than could the field-mice and wild flowers that surrounded him when Miss Austen drew his living portrait in 1811.

The extraordinary change from a village to an immense unbroken sea of bricks and mortar, occurring in the short space of little more than a century—a rate of change unequalled in any other historical period—is directly attributable to science. Had science not existed and, even more important, had the driving, restless and acquisitive people of the day not wished to apply it, the historical development of society would have been entirely different. In other times and other places, in the Syracuse where Archimedes lived, in the Italy of Leonardo da Vinci, in China where gunpowder was invented and used for the manufacture of fire-crackers, knowledge was available but was not necessarily applied to practical, material ends. But in Western Europe and America scientific knowledge was available *and* it was used. The knowledge and the use, starting slowly with the steam engine and the first iron machinery for spinning and weaving in the eighteenth century, came together in a gradually increasing flood in the nineteenth century, a flood which is still in full spate.

Man, in spite of his intellectual powers, his civilisation and culture, is an animal species and, as other living creatures do, must obey the laws of biology. One of the basic principles of biology is that whenever a species finds itself in a favourable environment, the numbers of that species increase. A simple example to consider is a bacteriological culture. If one takes an inoculum of any particular type of bacteria—a few million individuals, let us say, on a wire loop—and transfers it into a flask of warm broth, the bacteria, finding the environment favourable, begin to multiply.

The rate of increase of the population will be dependent on a number of factors: on the temperature, perhaps on the supply of oxygen, and, most important of all, on the particular kind of organism. One bacteria becomes two and then the two become four and the four eight. It can be seen that although the gestation period may remain constant the rate at which the population increases—what the bacteriologist calls the 'mean generation time'—becomes faster and faster. This is the so-called 'logarithmic' phase. Soon, however, the supply of oxygen, let us say, becomes barely sufficient for the needs of the growing numbers of organisms and each one, instead of finding a ready supply of nutrient broth at hand, has to go out, as it were, and search for sustenance. When this happens, the rate of multiplication slows down until at last it may happen that the rate at which new cells are produced is only sufficient to replace the rate at which old ones die. When this happens, the population has become stable. However, if at this stage conditions change and a new supply of broth is added, the numbers will again start to rise.

What I have described is, of course, an over-simplified model. Under normal circumstances a species seldom grows in isolation. The environment of the hippopotamuses in West Africa is partly made up of the rivers and lakes and the vegetation growing in and round them on which the animals feed. But it includes as well lions which kill the young hippopotamuses and farmers who kill the lions. If the farmers kill too many lions in order to protect their cattle, this operates as a favourable factor in the environment of the hippopotamuses, their numbers increase and they, in turn, become a nuisance to the farmers by trampling down the crops. The whole system, colloquially called 'the balance of Nature', is more precisely described as the science of ecology.

Human populations are as equally subject to the principles of ecology as populations of bacteria or hippopotamuses. A small 'inoculum' of Pilgrim Fathers introduced into the continent of North America soon found—after overcoming the comparatively sparse and primitive population of Red Indians—the environment favourable and multiplied until they became a nation. In the last hundred years, the favourable factor which has affected the human environment has been science. The application of genetics has led to the development of strains of wheat and maize which are far more productive than anything known before; hens have been bred to lay 300 eggs a year instead of the two or three clutches which were previously their best attainment; cows produce gallons of milk almost all the year round. But the most important of all has been the general influence of technology. The machines which have made transport faster and more certain; the engines which provide the motive power for all sorts of manufacture in place of muscle power; and, most recent of all, the computers which 'think' and control the organisation of whole factories: all these and many more have, in truth, saved human labour and, by making one man as effective as a thousand were before, enormously relieved the pressures and strains by which he was formerly burdened. This is to say, the human environment has suddenly through the applications of science become more favourable to the human species. And this has produced the result which any competent biologist could have predicted.

In the year 1800, the population of the earth was about 750 million. By 1850, it had become 1,000 million. After another fifty years it was more than 1,500 million, and by 1950 the number had reached 2,400 million. In the hundred years from 1850 to 1950 the population of the world had, therefore, increased nearly two and a half times. The human species was undergoing a period of exponential growth and in this increase in numbers the historical age, the life and manners of which Miss Austen wrote in 1816 were swept away.

Science has always been international. That is to say, although men of different nationalities have discovered the new knowledge and worked out the laws by which the different aspects of Nature are controlled, this knowledge has been made available to any scholar who wished to study it. At the beginnings of modern science in the seventeenth and eighteenth centuries, scientists were accustomed to write to each other or to communicate their discoveries by writing to the Royal Society in London or to some other centre of learning. Later on, specialised journals appeared in which they could describe their experiments and observations and discuss the conclusions which they drew from them. In view of this ready availability of scientific knowledge, it is of considerable historical interest to see that the eagerness to *use* such knowledge for practical ends was different in different countries. And even more subtle is the observation that within a single community enthusiasm for the idea of trying to apply new discoveries to develop fresh technological innovations has been by no means steady but has waxed and waned as the years passed. These phenomena are well demonstrated in the history of technology in Great Britain.

Britain was the first country to embrace science, apply it to technology and thus initiate the so-called 'Industrial Revolution'. The social results of this revolution were dramatic. In 1712, Thomas Newcomen and John Cawley built a 'fire engine'—what we should now call a steam engine—which could be used to pump water out of coal-mines far more effectively than could be done with horses. Neither Newcomen nor Cawley was a scientist: Newcomen was a blacksmith and Cawley a financier who had made his money by cattle dealing. But their engine made use of a scientific observation: that of Otto von Guericke, Burgomaster of Magdeburg, a rich amateur scientist who in 1650 made the first vacuum pump. His most dramatic experiment was to show that if the air was pumped out of a hollow brass ball about 18 inches in diameter and made in two halves, the vacuum produced would hold the two hemispheres together so firmly that sixteen horses—eight a side—could not pull them apart. The idea of using this 'force' of a vacuum to do work had been suggested by a Frenchman, Denis Papin, at the end of the seventeenth century. Papin had worked with the distinguished Dutch scientist, Christian Huygens—who conceived the clock pendulum, an improved telescope and the wave theory of light as well as studying the nature of vacuum —and later on collaborated with the equally famous Irish nobleman, the Honourable Robert Boyle. The combination of these great men whose names are remembered after three centuries testifies to how few scientists there were at the beginning of the modern scientific age. But Papin, although capable of comprehending the scientific principles involved, was unable to master the technological difficulties: his machine would not work satisfactorily. The Newcomen engine, although it only converted into work 1·2 per cent of the energy of the coal it burned, was an immediate success. The British mine-owners clamoured for it. The successful application of science to the technical problem of pumping not only prevented the mines from flooding but enabled them to be greatly extended and made twice as deep.

The principle of the Newcomen pump was to fill the cylinder with steam; during this time the piston rose and the rod, connected at the other end of a great beam to the pump in the mine below, was depressed; a spray of cold water was then injected into the cylinder, the steam was instantly condensed and the force of the vacuum thus produced sucked down the piston and worked the pump. Important though the Newcomen engine was to the history of coal-mining, its value was restricted because of its low efficiency: it needed so much coal to keep it going that it was used for very little else but coal-mine work. Sixty years later, in the 1770s, James Watt successfully applied a second and more refined scientific principle—that of the latent heat of steam, discovered by Joseph Black, professor of chemistry at the University of Glasgow where Watt had been employed as an instrument mechanic—and a steam engine efficient enough for general application was developed. The principal innovation developed by Watt was to draw off the latent heat of the steam, not by injecting cold water into the cylinder of the engine itself but by installing a separate condenser specially for the purpose.

The effect of this combination of scientific knowledge and the strong urge to use it and translate it into technological achievement—it took Watt alone from 1758 to 1787, a period of twenty-nine years' painstaking effort, to launch the steam engine as a practical proposition—was profound. The factory of Boulton and Watt supplied the mines and a growing industry with prodigious motive power. Britain quickly became the leading industrial nation in the world. New methods of production were developed. The power of a steam engine was distributed throughout a factory by a system of shafts, pulleys and belts and workpeople were gathered from the countryside and the villages to man the machines in them. Goods were made more cheaply than had been possible before and were distributed throughout the world. The steam engine was soon applied to transport and, in the form of the steam locomotive, revolutionised the movement of coal, food and goods of all sorts which had been previously dependent on waggons and sailing ships. In the course of a century, the power of the steam engine changed the whole of society. Production was enormously increased; coal, iron and steel, manufactured articles of all sorts could be made cheaper, more numerous and varied. In the eighteenth century, while this technological metamorphosis was gestating but before it had actually happened, British social life was much like that in many other European countries. By 1820, the country had become different from anywhere else on earth. Factories for spinning thread and other factories for weaving cloth, worked by steam engines, made textiles for the whole world. Iron foundries and engineering works blackened the face of the land. Smoky industrial towns sprang up in what a few years earlier were green fields. A bleak agglomeration of brick houses in row after row of featureless streets surrounded the huge factories to house the people drawn into the towns to work. The stability of the social structure, the nobility above, the landed gentry next and the working classes below, was broken. Industrialists and financiers grown rich were superseding the nobility and gentry but without having any responsibility for the 'detribalised' workpeople, uprooted from their birthplace, who came to live and work in the new towns. Dickens's satirical verse had a cruel topical bite:

> Oh let us have our occupations,
> Bless the squire and his relations,
> Live upon our daily rations,
> And always know our proper stations.

The social change had come, derived partly from the idea that technological improvement was possible and desirable; but the essential foundation of the magnitude and completeness of the change was the new discoveries of science. Science is knowledge of the workings of Nature, invention is the construction of a novel device to do some practical thing. Both are needed together if technology is to advance; and invention is limited when scientific understanding is lacking. In the Great Britain of the early nineteenth century, the essential significance of science was forgotten. The iron-masters and the cotton spinners, even the wealthy soap boilers and manufacturers of heavy chemicals forgot that their technology was based on science. They came to believe that their prosperity was solely based on financial judgement and business acumen. Their sons were educated to fit them to rule workmen, not to understand natural science. And the dynamism passed in Europe largely to Germany.

The Germans had understood what the 'British miracle' of the early nineteenth century was due to. And they learned from what they understood. Soon almost every head of a major industrial enterprise was a Herr Doktor. Soon the great British names of Newcomen, Watt, Black and Stevenson were matched and overtaken by the names of Rudolf Diesel, Karl Gauss, Werner Siemens, Justin von Liebig and Robert Bunsen. The most striking example of the way in which the flagging British technological drive was outpaced by the acceleration of the same movement in Germany is that of dyes.

W. H. Perkin almost accidently—but with the genius to recognise the significance of the accident—discovered the aniline dye, mauvine, and patented his discovery in 1856, when still a boy of eighteen. His father and brother helped him to set up in business and in 1874 he had made enough money from his dyes to be able to retire at the age of thirty-five. But it was not British scientists but German ones who developed other and more versatile dyes from the chemical principles discovered by Perkin. And from these the German chemists developed a variety of synthetic drugs as well. When in 1914, World War I began, the British and their allies found that the entire science-based industry, begun so dramatically by the young English Perkin, had become a German one and had to be rebuilt afresh before uniforms could be dyed, sick men treated and new explosives manufactured.

The historical period in which we live is different from anything that has gone before. The world is smaller and more crowded. A man can fly in indoor clothes from Copenhagen to Los Angeles across the North Pole. And side by side with this and other examples of new technology are signs of parallel changes in the organisation of society. These come about because the technological innovations based on science change men's ideas about life, death and disease, about the conduct of war, the production of food and wealth. These changes have taken place largely within the period between the Great Exhibition of 1851 and the present time: this has been the science century.

In particular the advances during our own lifetime have been of staggering magnitude. Does this imply that change which is so striking a feature of the present technological age is going to continue indefinitely and at an ever increasing pace? Or does a closer look at the history of this age of innovation suggest that there must be an end to such breathtaking changes and that the time when the science revolution will finish and humanity will enter a new phase may not—in historical terms—be long delayed?

Let us consider the speed of travel. It is only about a hundred years ago that man first succeeded in moving faster than the speediest animal—a horse. Today, millions of people fly at 600 m.p.h., plans are being made to produce commercial aeroplanes capable of flying at 2,000 m.p.h. and experimental rocket ships have achieved 4,000 m.p.h. We can assert with confidence that such increases in performance cannot continue indefinitely. At a speed of 17,000 m.p.h. the ultimate in air travel is reached because planes cease to fly and go into orbit.

The application of electromagnetism to spoken communications—as the telephone—was a great achievement of our grandparents. Today, we have radio and television—plain or coloured—with transmission all round the world by means of communications satellites. The development of immediate communications for everyone everywhere is already physically within our grasp.

Little more than a century ago, mechanical power was only just being applied to problems of the production of goods which previously had had to be made by human muscle power. Today, not only is power produced mechanically—from coal or oil or nuclear energy—not only do we have mass-production dependent on the detailed division of complex processes into simple parts but electronic computers, operating at high speeds, control the operation of entire factories. Already we are within sight of having solved the age-old need to work: in the post-science century, the problem will be instead that of leisure. And leisure substantially free from the fear of disease. Already, bacterial diseases are approaching extinction and virus diseases are coming under control. Cancer and circulatory disease are under attack and, although still constituting a serious problem, are likely to yield to scientific pressure in the foreseeable future.

The history of the past century when combined with that of the century still to come, while we cannot foresee its end, is certainly the bridge between two quite different kinds of human society. It is given to us to live—perhaps precariously—on this bridge and to be able to recognise it for what it is.

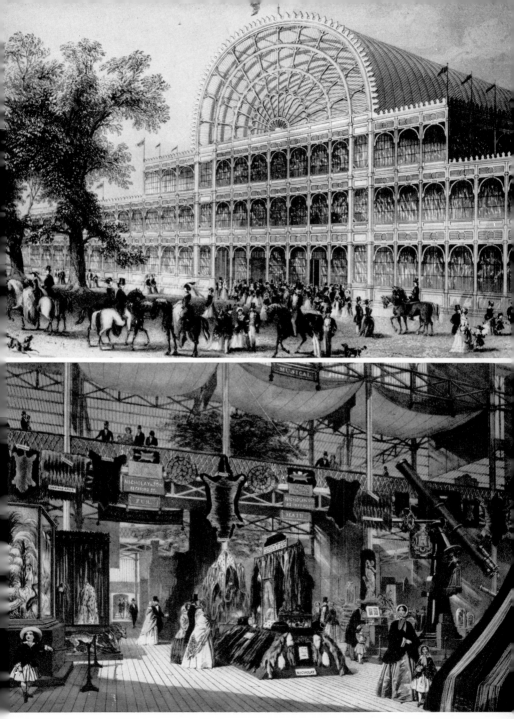

1: The Crystal Palace, 1851. Advanced technology in the age of horses. 2: The Great Exhibition—shop window of a new age.

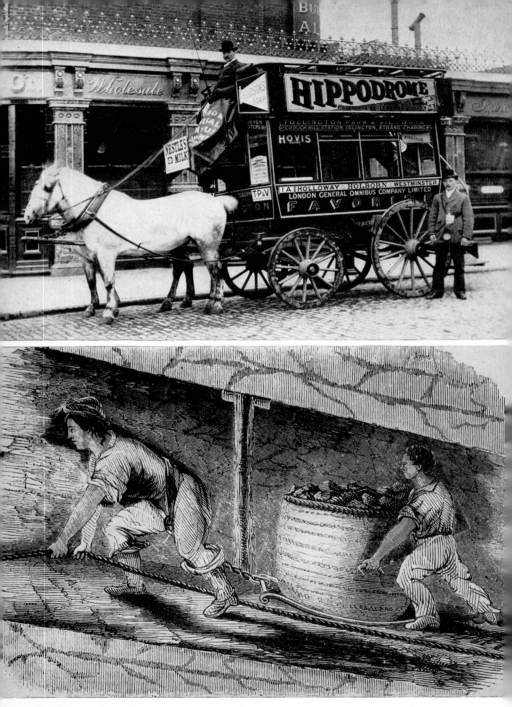

3: The omnibus of 1902, last word in horse-drawn public transport.   4: Coal-mining, 1842. The basic source of power for the nineteenth-century industrial economy. And it was reasonable to hire 'labour' at the cheapest rate.

6: The telephone, which annihilated distance and changed the time-scale of civilisation.

5: L. J. M. Daguerre, whose 'daguerreotypes' opened the door to modern photography and photo-copying and brought engraving to an end.

7: The retail distribution of food before bacteriology was discovered.

CHAPTER II

LIFE AND DEATH

In the world of 1850, when Dickens brought out *David Copperfield*, there was little to do if one's wife fell ill—presumably with tuberculosis—than to hope for her recovery and to watch her die.

My pretty Dora! . . . I began to carry her down-stairs every morning and up-stairs every night. She would clasp me round the neck and laugh, the while, as if I did it for a wager. . . . My aunt, the best and most cheerful of nurses, would trudge after us, a moving mass of shawls and pillows. . . . But, sometimes, when I took her up, and felt that she was lighter in my arms, a dead blank feeling came upon me, as if I were approaching to some frozen region yet unseen, that numbed my life. . . .

How the time wears, I know not. . . . 'Oh, Agnes! Look, look, here!' That face, so full of pity, and of grief, that rain of tears, that awful mute appeal to me, that solemn hand upraised towards Heaven! 'Agnes?' It is over. Darkness comes before my eyes.

The literature of the times a hundred years ago is full of sad death-bed scenes. The gravestones in any churchyard still tell of children carried off in their youth by consumption and a dozen other infectious diseases. The women of the mid-nineteenth century may have borne big families, but many of them could boast that they had 'buried seven'.

To glance at the pages of Dickens is to realise how complete has been the change in the historical climate between his time and our own. Today, the sick young wife would not be at home tended by her own husband and her husband's aunt. She would be in a hospital or sanatorium. Today, the 'dead, blank feeling' of hopelessness would be kept at bay by fresh air and—most potent of all—knowledge. The death rate* from tuberculosis, which was 5·7 in 1851–60, had become 0·5 in 1951 and tuberculosis hospitals were closed or converted to other uses.

Consider the state of medicine in 1837 when William Jenner took

* The figures given are the 'comparative mortality index' which makes allowance for the numbers of different sexes and ages in the population.

his diploma at the Apothecaries Hall in London. He was in his day exceptionally well trained having, like Bob Sawyer and Ben Allan, the fictional medical students in the *Pickwick Papers*, attended the medical school in Gower Street. Yet the tools of his trade were restricted to a wooden stethoscope and a scalpel for blood-letting. The clinical thermometer had not been invented when he qualified as a doctor. For the execution of the duties of his first appointment—as assistant physician at the London Fever Hospital—he had no effective drugs and only his skill as an observer to guide his practice. Of the hospital, Dickens wrote in the *Daily News*, 'The dread of infection worked within its walls as well as outside.' The first apothecary appointed at an annual salary of £30 refused to serve. The first porter decamped. The matron died within a year. When the place was rebuilt the local Vestry protested for fear lest the paupers in the parochial workhouse contiguous to the hospital should be infected.

Within the hospital were hopeless wretches abandoned by their families for fear of contagion rather than in expectation of cure. The sick were dirty, verminous and malodorous—indeed, the smell 'as of a wet umbrella' was used as a diagnostic sign of typhus. The distinction between different diseases, between typhus carried by lice and typhoid distributed by contaminated water, food or drink, even between these and diphtheria, erysipelas and measles was blurred. The doctor could only observe, lay his hands on the patient to assess his temperature and then pronounce the illness either a 'slow nervous fever' or a 'putrid fever'. And even the difference between these two kinds was not clear and one might, it was thought, change into the other. Only smallpox had been identified as a separate entity on account of its particularly severe and disfiguring character and because nearly a century before William Jenner's great namesake, Edward Jenner, had discovered the efficiency of vaccination with cowpox virus—and was in due time rewarded with a vote of £30,000 by the British Parliament for freeing his own land and, indeed, the world from one of its most destructive and fearful scourges. The best that William Jenner could do—and it was a substantial contribution in its time—was to recognise that typhus, also called 'jail' or 'camp' fever, one of the major killing diseases, was a different disease from typhoid. He did not know the cause of either nor could he administer any cure other than patience and hope; but to distinguish between them, to observe that a man with typhus had an expression of drunkenness whereas a patient with typhoid appeared dull, dreary and apathetic—this at least was the beginning of medical knowledge in the early years of the nineteenth century.

The lack of scientific knowledge a century ago affected the rich and well educated equally with the poor. The precarious tenure of life of the overcrowded working people in the sordid dwellings of the industrial towns—houses without bathrooms, ideally suited for the transmission of lice and hence of typhus—was a feature of the historical background of the period. Napoleon's casualties on the Beresina River were as much due to typhus as to the cold winter and the Russian forces. Even if well-to-do people suffered less frequently than their social inferiors the annoyance of lice and hence the risk of typhus, they were equally susceptible to typhoid. Their drinking water was equally likely to be contaminated. The tradesmen and servants who handled their food could in all ignorance contaminate it with *Salmonella typhi*, the existence of which was then unknown. How should they know that their unwashed hands after obeying the calls of nature, might be lethally contaminated?

In December 1861 the Prince Consort, then forty-four years old, became unwell with a 'slow fever'. His doctors had no means of making any precise diagnosis, there were no blood tests to do, no way of identifying the causative agent, the very idea that microorganisms gave rise to disease had not been conceived. Two doctors were in attendance on the Prince, Sir James Clark and William Jenner, but they did not really know what was the matter with him. He was not even put to bed, but for days lay listlessly on a sofa while Queen Victoria read to him. It was some time before his condition was diagnosed as 'fever'. He did not have any expert nursing; Florence Nightingale's missionary work had primarily applied to conditions in the army abroad and nurses, for the most part, were uneducated and untrained. Even when it was clear that the Prince was seriously ill, he was still permitted to get up and walk about his dressing-room. There were no hospitals to which he could be sent where conditions could be expected to be better than those of Windsor Castle: on the contrary, to enter a hospital at all was to undergo serious risk of further infection in the world of 1861.

After a month, the Queen was told 'in the kindest and clearest manner' that the Prince Consort had 'fever'. But even then, when the diagnosis had been made, the prescription to be followed was that the illness must be allowed to take its course and that there was no cause for alarm.

And so the illness, now recognised to be typhoid fever, did take its course in that so different world of a century ago, a world within a generation of the scientific elucidation of bacteriology, of the elaboration of hygienic principles based on bacteriology and of the development of bacteriocidal agents to control the disease-causing organisms. The Prince's condition became still more grave. He was moved to another bedroom. But still he got up to be wheeled into a sitting-room where Princess Alice played to him on the piano. He developed 'congestion of the lungs'. More doctors were called in. The Prince assisted by a valet and a page, was helped into another bed. His lips became blue and his face dusky and pallid. On December the 14th, 1861, the Queen was called into the sick-room. The Prince's left hand was already cold and his breathing was feeble. An hour later, surrounded by his family, he died.

History, according to the *Concise Oxford Dictionary*, is 'the continuous methodical record of public events, the study of the growth of nations and the whole train of events connected with nations, persons and things'. One of the greatest events in the history of modern society has surely been the change in people's apprehension of disease and hence of life and death. Individuals no longer feel themselves to be subject to the sport and caprice of gods or devils or the evil eye. No longer do they fear that out of the blue and all of a sudden in the full prime of their manhood they may be struck down by a fever which they can do nothing to avoid or resist. It is true that modern middle-aged men may be carried off by lung cancer or coronary heart disease, but these men also know that when they work, eat and smoke too much—or, for that matter, travel too fast or too often in sports-cars—they run a risk by doing so. The universe is a different place for modern men because, for them, it is at least in part under their own control; for their ancestors it was a place of fearful and unmanageable things.

For nations as well, the scientific control of infectious diseases was a major historical landmark. Big cities, with their concentration of industrial and political power, became safely possible. The control of malaria—the ague—threw open new lands at home and abroad— the marshy fen country of England, the Pontine Marshes around Rome and African territories for colonisation and conversion. And the fall in death rate affected events, firstly, by causing populations to increase and then, later on, when women no longer needed the sour boast that they had seen their children pine and die by bringing about smaller families of fewer, better-cared-for children. Perhaps the next result in the context of history is the gradual disappearance of the family group possessing its strong feeling of fellowship, and its replacement by one or perhaps two individuals who barely recognise their common parentage. The deathbed scene of Prince Albert is an anachronism in the twentieth century. Men and women no longer die at home surrounded by sorrowing friends and relations: instead, they die alone in hospitals under expert technical supervision. There is no place for wives and children when oxygen masks, transfusion bottles and, possibly, cardiac massage are wanted. The balance is in all realistic respects in favour of the twentieth century, which saves men of forty-four dying of typhoid and prevents most men of any age from contracting such a disease at all. Indeed, the progress of scientific medicine can clearly be seen to have changed the flavour of death.

Birth too has changed and is no longer a family event. Almost within our own generation, the children of technologically advanced nations have ceased to be born upstairs in the best bedroom. They are born, as they die, not among affectionate albeit incompetent friends and relations, but instead in the presence of qualified technologists. Even one's mother is nowadays sometimes unconscious at the time. And this is only possible because science has made hospitals safer than homes.

In the middle of the nineteenth century puerperal fever was so common in maternity hospitals that women in labour were, with good cause, too frightened for their lives to enter them. The cause of the fever was quite unknown: foods were suspected, even scents were at one time accused. Then the Hungarian physician, Ignaz-Philipp Semmelweiss, made the acute observation that some of the anatomical and pathological symptoms of an assistant who had died of an infection contracted during the course of a dissection were similar to those of women dying of childbed fever. From this he deduced that such fevers might also be due to an introduced infection. The facts supported this hypothesis. Deaths from puerperal fever were much commoner in clinics where the students and doctors did their obstetrics without washing their hands or taking any special precautions to keep the place clean.

The history of Semmelweiss' idea is an interesting one. He reported his conclusions to the Medical Council of Vienna and demonstrated their truth by the rapid fall in the number of women dying when his principles were accepted and where all who came in contact with women in labour washed their hands and where the wards were disinfected by chlorination.

'What experience and history teach is this,' wrote Hegel, 'that people and governments never have learned anything from history.' Put more succinctly, this asserts that all we learn from history is that we learn nothing from history. Part of the reason for this is the reluctance of men and women to accept new ideas that require them to change their preconceived ideas. The leading obstetricians in Vienna of the 1850s were convinced that their methods of practice as established over the years were good and could not be improved; the fact that women coming into hospital to have their babies died of fever did not affect the issue. In consequence of this rigid belief they opposed the new ideas of Semmelweiss; their attacks on his proposals were so violent that he was compelled to leave his post in Vienna. In 1855 he was appointed professor in the University of Budapest where, in 1861, he published the results of his work under the title, *On the aetiology, the pathology, and the prophylaxis of puerperal fever.*

It is important to remember that even in 1861 the science of bacteriology and the discoveries of Pasteur upon which it is based were still unknown. Although Semmelweiss had correctly observed the facts and although his deductions based on these facts—that infection was carried by dirty hands, and by unclean beds and lying-in rooms, and by the soiled frock coats of the doctors who moved from one patient to the next wearing their dignified and, as it now appears, unsuitable costumes—were correct, the reason why they were correct was still unknown. No one could believe that so ordinary an object as a dirty hand or a rumpled cuff could carry an invisible, harmful, living agent; and because they did not understand them, Semmelweiss' adversaries continued to deny the facts he showed them. Constant opposition eventually overcame him; he resigned his Chair and some years later he died with a deranged mind. His work, however, was done; in 1894, the city of Budapest erected a statue in his honour. The scientific discovery he made brought about the change in social history: the women of the twentieth century come together, as a 'natural' thing to do, to bear their babies in a community centre which, in the nineteenth century, only the most hard driven and unfortunate would have entered at her peril.

The changes in the entire attitude of men and women to birth, life and death—the major change in confidence and understanding that life and health were more likely to continue rather than come to an abrupt, capricious and fearful end, as well as the minor but nevertheless important change of the relaxation of the bonds of family at the beginning and end of life and their replacement by the technical ministrations of paid experts provided by the community—were due to science. One man can never be named the single discoverer of a major area of new knowledge. Scientists, like writers, artists and other creative people, are always members of a group who jointly engender the atmosphere from which discoveries arise. It is true, however, that within a group, one man may stand predominant. And if any single person can be chosen as the source of ideas which changed the whole practice of medicine, that man is Louis Pasteur.

The genius of Pasteur was that, as a scientist, he was armed at every point. He had the insight and wit to see new principles underlying the facts of observation and experiment; he had the skill and talent to design experiments and tests accurately aimed to verify a selected and particular conclusion; he had luck above his deserts but, at the same time, the intellectual agility and flexibility to deserve the luck he had; and he possessed the drive, vigour and determination to overcome and finally convince his opponents.

Louis Pasteur's history has often been told but it is worth retelling. His work established a scientific principle of general application, and for this reason his discoveries not only led to such things as he himself achieved, the effective treatment of anthrax and rabies, triumphs though these were indeed. They also provided the illumination by which other men could see how to deal with infectious diseases in general. Edward Jenner could prevent smallpox by his discovery, but smallpox alone because, though he found out vaccination with cowpox, he did not fathom the principles of immunology. Chadwick halted the typhoid epidemic that ravaged London by taking off the handle of the Aldgate pump. He observed that the disease was transmitted by water but failed to discover the pathological principle the contaminated water carried.

At every stage of his career, Pasteur had the genius to see more than the results of the experiments he did; he could also recognise

21

the basic causes of what was happening. In 1848, when he was a young man of twenty-six, he observed the *reason* why a sample of the chemical compound, tartaric acid, prepared from wine lees deviated a ray of polarised light to the right whereas tartaric acid, with the identical chemical components but prepared from the so-called 'mother liquors' of cream of tartar, did not; he saw that this second acid when crystallised formed two kinds of crystals, differing only in being, as it were, geometrical mirror-images of each other. Pasteur showed that if one took the trouble to separate all the right-handed crystals from the left-handed crystals and dissolved them separately in water, both solutions deflected polarised light, but one deflected it to the left and the other to the right.

This discovery was interesting and, at the time it was made, surprising and unexpected to the organic chemists of the day. But Pasteur went further. He conceived the idea that chemical compounds which possess the extraordinary ability to deflect polarised light—which possess, that is, non-symmetrical molecular configuration—are products of biological processes. He saw a similarity with the one-sided twist of plant tendrils which follow the sun, or with the cork-screw thread of sea shells. Tartaric acid, derived from wine lees, is a product of fermentation. Amyl alcohol, which Pasteur subsequently isolated from grain-alcohol, also deflects polarised light and is also a fermentation product. His deduction, therefore, was that fermentation was not a chemical process, as had until then been believed, but was a biological one and that it was due to the life processes of yeasts.

It is hardly important whether the twisting of polarised light is due to life processes or not: modern scientists give little thought to the matter. But Pasteur's generalisation was, right or wrong, enormously fruitful. He demonstrated conclusively that fermentation by which beer is produced is indeed due to living yeast and that the alcohol that results is a life-product. He also showed, in the teeth of prolonged and weighty opposition, that life is only begotten from life and that spontaneous generation does not occur. To do this he exhibited experimental talent of the highest order. But note the genius of the man in establishing again a general principle: living creatures—whether or not they are microscopic yeast cells or bluebottle maggots, popularly supposed in the 1850s to be generated from putrid meat—are *only* derived from other living creatures, their parents.

At every stage, Pasteur's career illustrates the potency of scientific

22

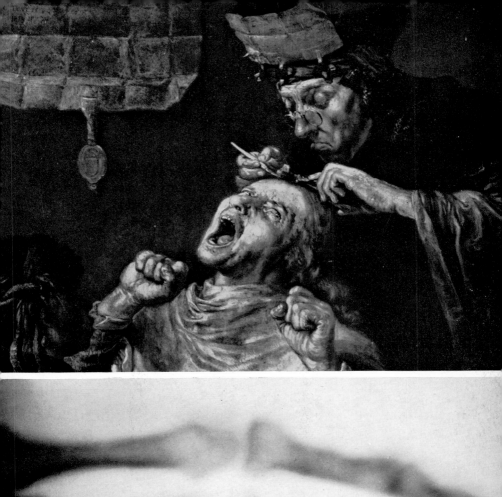

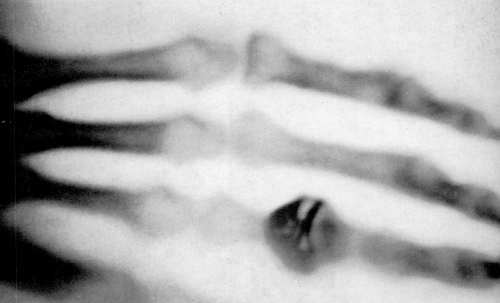

8: Surgery before anaesthetics was not so far removed from this symbolic picture of 'The excision of follies', attributed to Jan de Bray. 9: The first X-ray picture from which much modern diagnosis and treatment stem.

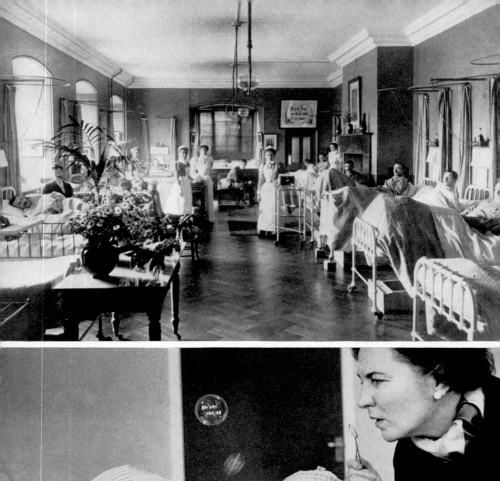

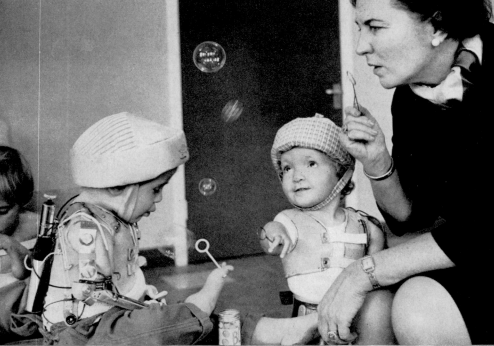

10: Hospital wards remained much the same during the advance of scientific medicine. 11: Thalidomide, an excellent tranquilliser, brought disaster to the unborn babies of women who took it in early pregnancy. Now others care for them. Knowledge is never complete.

generalisations. It might at a superficial glance be thought that studies of *dextro-* and *laevo*-tartaric acid, the two sorts one of which deflects polarised light to the right and the other to the left, while an interesting curiosity for an academic organic chemist are of little significance to busy men of affairs. It could be argued that investigations into beer fermentation, while of possible value to brewers, are hardly matters of interest to ladies and gentlemen of good education. Yet the general principles of science which describe the way that Nature works are, almost of all matters, of greatest importance to a civilised community.

From the conception that fermentation was a manifestation of life, combined with the principle which he also established that all living creatures are the descendants of their ancestors, Pasteur was led to deduce that 'sick' beer and wine, that is liquor that had become spoiled by the conversion of the original sugar, not into alcohol but into lactic acid, must be due to the presence of another living creature different from yeast. Pasteur's opponents again denied his theories. Yeast was undoubtedly seen to grow and multiply as the alcohol increased in the fermenting wine or beer, but lactic acid in the sour, spoiled liquor was another matter. Justin von Liebig, the distinguished German chemist, denied that yeasts were the cause of fermentation for the very reason that confirmed Pasteur in his conviction that they were. Von Liebig admitted that the microscopic globules of yeast were present in fermenting liquor but asserted that no such bodies were present when fermentations 'went wrong' and produced lactic acid. Pasteur looked more searchingly and recognised the much smaller, elongated shapes of lactic-acid-producing bacteria.

At every stage Pasteur demonstrated his skill as well as his insight. He developed methods which enabled him to isolate and grow the organisms which produced lactic acid and other organisms which produced amyl alcohol. This showed him that different kinds of 'germs' behaved in different ways and produced different end results. He soon demonstrated his talent for applying the scientific principles he was elucidating in practical ways. He was consulted by Monsieur Bigo, the owner of a distillery at Lille, to find a way to prevent his fermentations becoming 'sick' and slimy. Pasteur installed a microscope and taught the distillery chemist to distinguish between the spherical or oval appearance of yeast in uncontaminated fermentations from which good yields of alcohol would be obtained and the rod-shaped organisms which would spoil the fermentation by producing acid.

The appreciation that the presence of specific types of 'microbes' produce distinctive kinds of 'sickness' in beer or wine led Pasteur to the notion that they could equally well be the cause of different diseases. And his handling of the practical problems of industry about which he was consulted provided him with apt precedents when later on he was faced with problems of disease. In 1863 he was asked his advice on how best the French wine industry could cope with the 'diseases' of sour, bitter and cloudy fermentations by which the producers were plagued. Pasteur observed that on each occasion these conditions were due to the presence of unwanted micro-organisms. He proposed two solutions, simple yet profound. The first, to prevent wine from becoming vinegary, was to adjust the acidity by adding potash and thus make the conditions more favourable to the yeast, which could thus outgrow and overcome the infecting bacteria. His second solution was to heat the wine sufficiently to kill the bacteria causing the spoilage: the process is called 'pasteurisation' to this day. Already, therefore, to maintain the 'health' of his beer and wine, he was, on the one hand, increasing the ability of the body of fermenting liquor to resist infection and, on the other hand, applying means to destroy invading micro-organisms.

In 1856 Pasteur was studying the disease anthrax, which is lethal to pigs and sheep and can also infect people. Acting on the principle that the complaint was caused by a micro-organism, he set out to identify it and, when he had done so in the blood of infected animals, he isolated it and grew it in broth in his laboratory. To prove that his isolated cultures really were the cause of anthrax, he used them to infect healthy animals artificially.

Then he took thought. He was of course aware of Jenner's work. But rather than taking the fact that a previous attack of trivial cowpox acted as a protection against lethal smallpox as an isolated phenomenon he reflected whether there could be a general principle underlying it. So far as anthrax was concerned, there was no natural condition equivalent to cowpox known to counteract its attack. Could it be, however, that protection against infectious diseases in general was to be achieved by the stimulation of resistance? After all nobody contracts measles twice. Following this line of reasoning, Pasteur set out in his laboratory to damage the natural fatal vigour of his isolated anthrax cultures by growing the organisms under unfavourable conditions which, while allowing them to live and grow, might be expected to cripple them. Exercising his remarkable talents as an experimenter, one of the things he did was to grow the anthrax organisms at what was for them unnaturally hot temperatures. And this general technique was successful. The weakened culture injected into sheep, while it did not give them anthrax, successfully protected them against subsequent infection by wild strains of the disease germs. And in 1881, in a farmyard at Pouilly-le-Fort, he carried out his celebrated public experiment at which, with characteristic nineteenth-century panache—which, with our modern blasé familiarity with scientific 'miracles', we have largely lost—he demonstrated with twenty-two dead sheep and an equal number of living immunised ones, that science could appropriately be applied to medicine.

History describes what the life of a particular time and place is like. To look at a child in the England of the 1860s was to know that 2,282 out of each million would die from scarlet fever; from a million such children in the 1950s only 1 died of scarlet fever. In the 1860s, 1,122 children per million died from diphtheria; in the 1960s the number was 2. From the whole population, the 'comparative mortality index' for typhoid was 84·37 in the 1870s; in 1951, the figure had become 0·12—only one seven-hundredth the number of people died of the infection.

In 1850, medical science did not exist. Medicine was not a science at all. Although doctors in Europe might be trained at universities, in Great Britain to be a doctor a man had to serve an apprenticeship. The Royal Colleges which came largely to control medical practice in the nineteenth century in Britain were formed on the same basis as the ancient Guild Companies of craftsmen and merchants. The great majority of students and of the men who taught them learned their art by studying to pass the examinations of the Colleges. It is hardly surprising, therefore, that the transformation of medicine from an expert trade with a fixed system of tradition and practice into a branch of applied science—what we now call a technology—should have been brought about, partly by the general climate of science and technology as manifest by the new steam engines and looms and dyeworks, and partly by men like Pasteur, a chemist without medical training at all.

The germ theory was of all the scientific ideas applicable to medicine the most important. No one could fail to appreciate the greatness of Pasteur's discoveries and the practical achievement based on them. After him came other giants. Paul Ehrlich in Germany between 1877 and 1890 identified a wide variety of micro-organisms, some of which caused disease and some of which did not. He laid the foundations of the scientific understanding of immunology, first stumbled upon by Jenner and later established as a principle of disease resistance by Pasteur. But Ehrlich's most famous work was the introduction of the use of chemical dyes to differentiate between different types of cells and tissues and to elucidate their function. This led him to conceive the idea that chemical compounds of appropriate molecular structure might be synthesised which would be capable of combining with pathological micro-organisms and thus destroying them. This notion was the germ of what is today called *chemotherapy*. The drugs of pre-scientific medicine were derived from herbs and a wide variety of traditional and often quasi-superstitious sources. Ehrlich for the first time set himself to synthesise a therapeutic agent designed specifically to achieve a chosen purpose. The most celebrated of the compounds he prepared was No. 606, *salvarsan*, the cure for syphilis.

Robert Koch, another great German worker, refined and developed methods for handling micro-organisms and in large measure established bacteriology as an independent branch of biological science. He prepared pure cultures of the anthrax bacillus in 1876; in 1882 he isolated the bacillus of tuberculosis and two years later he identified the organism causing Asiatic cholera.

The climate of thought about life, death and disease was changed by the emergence of knowledge, understanding and system as the basis of action rather than tradition, faith and prayer. This is not to say that earlier beliefs had not led to action in the time before knowledge was available. Smollett in the eighteenth century wrote of the bleeding and purging that were then commonplace activities in clinical medicine—and, being a sensible Scotsman and a good observer as well, he wrote too of his suspicions that those drastic medical treatments might kill as many patients as they cured. Today, this end result, when it happens, is more politely termed *iatrogenic mortality*. In 1848 the British Public Health Act and the Nuisances Removal and Diseases Prevention Acts were passed and the General Board of Health established to implement them.

Just at the time the General Board of Health was set up, there was an outbreak of cholera in England which caused the death of 54,000 people. How radical has been the change in atmosphere in the short historical time which has elapsed since then. The Board of Health, while ignorant of the cause of the cholera, deduced that it was being transmitted by drinking water and by their vigorous actions introduced suitable precautions. A practical success, though valuable for its own sake, can hamper advance when it makes 'practical' men scornful of theoretical study. The achievement of the Board of Health led to a general identification of smells and 'nuisance' with infectivity. There was, to be sure, good reason to take pains to avoid smelly drains yet, even in the 1860s, to rip up the floor boards of Windsor Castle searching for drains as the cause of a bad smell—as, indeed, was done—could still lead to the true cause of typhoid being overlooked. The smell, it was later discovered, was due to an escape of gas.

Although the age of enlightenment, as we know it today, can be said to have begun in the seventeenth century with Newton as the great dominant Moses bringing illumination to what had previously been a state of scientific chaos, the first of the great discoveries were in physics and astronomy. Progress in the understanding of chemistry and, still more, in interpreting such understanding into something of practical usefulness, was delayed for almost two hundred years. The difficulty of chemistry, the science of the composition of matter, is that matter, in what we are accustomed to call its 'chemical' sense, is composed of ninety-two different kinds of stuff—the ninety-two elements. A novice can make quicker progress in music if he starts by learning to play the recorder which involves the sounding of only one note at a time. A piano with ninety-two keys is more difficult, particularly if—as was the state of chemistry at the beginning of the nineteenth century—the player has little idea of the order of the notes or the relation of one to another.

The great advances in chemical understanding—the new chemistry first glimpsed by Lavoisier at the end of the eighteenth century—had to wait for John Dalton in 1803 to invent a systematic way of codifying chemical reactions. Indeed, not until first Newlands in 1864 and then Mendeleev in 1869 brought order into the relationship of the elements and, almost literally, arranged the ninety-two 'notes' into the 'octaves' of the Periodic Table, could the modern age of chemical science be said to have begun. This period, it should be noted, is exactly the time when the great advances in scientific medicine were also occurring and, for the first time, the nature of infectious bacteria being understood and the way to control them worked out. It is not entirely surprising, therefore, that the discovery of anaesthetics—a side-result of progress in chemistry—took place in this same period of intellectual revolution. So familiar are we today with the idea that surgical operations are always carried out on insensible patients, that it requires a conscious effort of imagination to take ourselves back into the different period of history when surgeons, bloody to the elbow, prided themselves on the rapidity with which they could amputate a limb and patients, as drunk as they could get and strapped to a chair, suffered the agony they must as best they could.

It is curious to recall that although Sir Humphry Davy recognised the anaesthetic properties of nitrous oxide—'laughing gas'—as long ago as 1800 and, indeed, suggested its use during surgical operations, his proposal was not taken up. The idea of the inevitability of pain and suffering was so ingrained and, for that matter, so tangled with moral and religious ideas about the virtuous nature of endurance and fortitude on the one hand and the wrath and vengeance of God on the other, that something more than chemical knowledge was needed to bring about the relief of pain by so material and artificial a means as chemistry. At first, then, 'laughing gas' was an interesting scientific novelty, a mere example of Davy's dramatic ability to expound the new ideas of natural philosophy to a fashionable and appreciative audience at the Royal Institution in Albemarle Street. A few adventurous people might perhaps sniff the gas for fun to appreciate its strange physiological effect. Later on, Davy's great successor at the Royal Institution, Michael Faraday, inhaled ether and reported its effect. Even in 1842, when Crawford Long in America actually used ether to produce anaesthesia for a surgical operation, he did not make known what he had done; and two years later, in December 1844, when Horace Wells had nitrous oxide administered to himself before having a tooth out, the subsequent public demonstration was a fiasco. It was 1847 before James Simpson in Edinburgh successfully introduced chloroform as an anaesthetic.

Simpson was violently attacked from many quarters and the use of chloroform, particularly to mitigate suffering in childbirth was denounced as impious and contrary to Holy Writ. But besides bringing to an end the acute agonies of pre-scientific history which, for example, led Pepys to measure time from the year when he was 'cut for the stone', the dramatic introduction of anaesthetics from about 1850 and of antiseptics, to control bacterial infection, from about 1870 led to vast improvements in surgical technique.

Today, an attack of appendicitis, a mere inflammation of the large bowel, is little more than a trivial inconvenience requiring three or four weeks' absence from work for a citizen of any reasonably technologically advanced state. A hundred years ago, it could be a sentence of death. In the eighteenth century, a surgeon could amputate extremities, excise tumours on the surface of the body and remove stones from the urinary bladder—the operation Pepys found so excruciating. The scope of the surgeon's activities was only partly limited by the pain of operative procedures; another crucial limitation was the liability of the wound to an infection from which the patient all too often died. A hundred years ago, it was a bold surgeon who would open the abdomen, even if he could find a patient with sufficient fortitude to allow him to do so. In 1857, the commonest operations other than amputations were for breast tumours and strangulated hernia, from which last over half the patients operated upon died! At that time, according to a review presented to the British Medical Association, in a three-month period, of thirteen operations for stone in the bladder carried out in the hospitals of London, three patients died.

In 1867, Joseph Lister introduced his antiseptic method for the prevention of infection in wounds. This combined with the use of anaesthetics at last allowed the surgeon to extend his scope. By the end of the nineteenth century surgery using the chemistry of anaesthetics and the biology of infection—itself a discovery derived from Pasteur's scientific work (which also started as chemistry)—could save the life of many people who must otherwise have died. And in the twentieth century, chemistry has continued to assist the surgeon. Up to 1914 technique advanced to a remarkable degree. Sir Arbuthnot Lane brought asepsis, especially in dealing with complicated fractures, to a singularly high pitch by the use of his 'no touch' technique, in which nothing but the instruments were put in the wound. Indeed, so versatile did he become that he was tempted to remove portions of his patients on the general principle that it might do them good.

But the century's history of surgical advance, contributing to the revolution of the citizen's ideas of life and death, did not depend only on the sciences of chemistry and biology. Physics also played a major part. On Friday, November the 8th, 1895, Wilhelm Röntgen observed that the electromagnetic radiation of short wave-length with which he was experimenting caused a platinocyanide screen on a bench to show light in the dusk of the laboratory; seven weeks later he published a paper describing the phenomenon—and X-rays had been discovered. The first X-ray picture taken for clinical purposes was achieved by an electrical engineer, not a doctor; it was taken by Campbell Swinton on January the 7th, 1896.

We who see men flying round and round the globe in rockets have lost our sense of wonder. But to our grandparents, to see the bones through their covering of flesh, to localise fractures, to see—veritably to see—a safety-pin in a baby's oesophagus were marvels. And for the surgeon, to know precisely what he was to find and where before he made the incision was yet one more major change in history.

X-rays were first used to detect and localise foreign bodies. Then came the radiological demonstration of fractures; within ten years, tuberculosis could be investigated, diseases of the bone and bony tumours. By 1909, the alimentary tract could also be examined and gastric and duodenal ulcers detected.

In spite of the skill and virtuosity of the surgeons of the first two decades of the present century, in spite of the understanding of asepsis and the development of a variety of anaesthetics capable of maintaining patients for quite long periods in an anaesthetised state, death from wound infections continued to occur and achieved frightful proportions during World War I. The situation was radically changed, and people quickly recognised that it had changed, when in 1927, a Scottish pathologist working in St Mary's Hospital, London, observed that the growth of the pathogenic staphylococci which he was culturing in his laboratory was checked by the presence of a mould which had accidentally contaminated one of his preparations. Fleming had the wit to see the implications of this chance happening. He prepared from cultures of the mould a filtrate which he found to be capable of inhibiting the growth not only of staphylococci but of many other types of bacteria as well.

It took nearly twenty years, first for Fleming and then Howard Florey, an Australian, and Ernest Chain, who was born in Germany, to isolate the active material—penicillin—and then for manufacturers to find means of producing it on a large scale, before it became available generally. By that time a series of other potent agents, streptomycin, aureomycin, terromycin, each capable of inhibiting different kinds of infective bacteria, had been discovered. These biologically produced agents, known collectively as antibiotics, together with the chemotherapeutic compounds of which the sulphonamides were the first, have brought within sight the end of infectious disease as something which people believe they have to fear.

But far though the achievements of the science century may have gone, there are signs as the century ends that the command over human ills which they represent will never be complete. Let us, in concluding this chapter, consider malaria.

Of all the ills that have afflicted mankind, few have taken a higher toll than malaria. Throughout history it has continued its ravages. In the Middle Ages, epidemics occurred as deadly as the plague. Even today in the second half of the twentieth century, it defies complete suppression. After World War I, a devastating outbreak struck the Soviet Union; 5 million cases were reported and deaths in the one year, 1923, were more than 60,000. In Brazil, where a new species of mosquito was introduced from Africa in 1938, 100,000 cases occurred and 14,000 people died. It was in the 1890s, in the first flowering of scientific effort, that Ronald Ross, an army surgeon in India, discovered that the plasmodium parasite which causes the disease was transported by the *Anopheles* mosquitoes. Ross's investigations, followed by those of Grassi in Italy, elucidated the main facts, but only in 1948 did Shortt and Garnham working in London complete the story by their discovery that for part of their life-cycle the organisms penetrate into the liver of a sufferer from malaria.

Once scientific investigation had showed that malaria was spread by *Anopheles* mosquitoes, ways of stopping the disease could be planned. At first, the attack was directed towards draining the wet places where the mosquito larvae breed or treating them with larvicides. This, though it had a direct effect on history (it made the Panama Canal possible), was only partially successful. In 1935, two South African workers, Park-Ross and Meillan, showed that it was more effective to tackle the mosquitoes themselves with fly sprays. In 1938, DDT was discovered and it seemed that the battle was won, particularly when a series of even more potent insecticides—chlordane, dieldrin, malathion and many others—were developed by chemical researchers. These new scientific discoveries revolutionised the

31

situation. By treating the paint on their walls with DDT or one of the other new insecticides houses could be made lethal to mosquitoes and malaria-safe for the people living in them.

To protect people outside their houses, new synthetic drugs, proguanil, pyrimethamine, prevent the plasmodium reaching the liver; mepacrine and chloroquine attack the plasmodium when it enters the blood cells—and there are many more. Yet in spite of the knowledge and the technology and wealth which enables the scientific agents to be applied, and in spite of radio communications and a worldwide effort mounted by the World Health Organisation, although the success is very great it is still not complete.

The world is a different place from what it was a hundred years ago. Few people die of typhoid. Surgery, previously impossible, can be done safely and without pain. Organs can be removed and replaced, the heart itself can be stitched while the blood is circulated by a mechanical pump and oxygenated in an artificial 'lung', the brain can be repaired. Yet even while the great new discoveries of the complex nature of malaria were being unravelled and elegant scientific solutions applied to the problems as, one by one, they were elucidated, first there began to appear mosquitoes which were resistant to DDT and chlordane and the rest, and then there were found plasmodia that can survive mepacrine and chloroquine and even quinine.

It seems that just as the lessons of history are that the great political prizes of liberty and justice, comfort and learning are only gained at the price of constant vigilance and effort, so also are the scientific prizes of command over disease and early death.

CHAPTER III

WAR AND PEACE

War is perhaps the technology which, of all others, men have studied most carefully and for longest. A hundred years ago, therefore, a considerable degree of technological versatility had already been superimposed on the art of fighting. Even so, the hundred years of fertile science from the mid-nineteenth to the mid-twentieth century brought about some remarkable changes in military science, that is, the process of imposing political decisions by force.

The technique of war—if, for the moment we restrict our discussion to dry land—can be divided roughly into three main operations. First is the killing of one man by another directly, face to face. There is little science in this operation and the technique has changed hardly at all throughout recorded history: a modern soldier equipped with a bayonet would find himself quite at home in a battlefield of classical times, as he would at Agincourt. In spite of what army instructors may say, the operation of sticking a spear into another man or striking him with a heavy instrument is comparatively simple. The second operation, the use of cavalry, or elephants, or heavy tanks, however, has undergone significant modification and improvement through the years due to the advent of scientific methods: a modern armoured vehicle would have little difficulty in coping with Boadicea's chariot. The third main technique of war, the casting of projectiles, owes perhaps most of all to science.

Let us for the moment defer consideration of the basic theoretical studies which exercised some of the most brilliant scientific minds of earlier centuries in elucidating the fundamental mathematics underlying the flight of a projectile, whether it be an arrow, the bolt from a crossbow—itself a remarkable technical advance in its time—or a ball shot from a cannon; let us consider the state of knowledge a century or so ago, at the beginning of the short period of history we are discussing.

The battle of Borodino, between Napoleon's forces and those of Czar Alexander, was fought on September the 7th, 1812. The French and Russian armies were drawn up approximately 2,000 yards apart. It was Napoleon's intention that a concentration of 102 guns should open fire and shower shells on the Russian forces. In the event, as pointed out by Tolstoy in his vivid account of the engagement, this could not be done, as from the spots selected by Napoleon—who had a heavy cold at the time—the projectiles did not carry to the Russian lines, and these 102 guns shot into the air until the nearest commander, contrary to Napoleon's instructions, moved them forward. That is to say, in 1812, although excellent artillery was available, its effective range was less than 2,000 yards. The battle itself, although replete with prototypes of the same technological devices we use today, and as murderous as modern war, seems now almost as different as a fairy story. Consider some of Tolstoy's descriptions.

Pierre [a Russian Count] went down the street to the knoll from which he had looked at the field of battle the day before. It was the same panorama . . . but now the whole place was full of troops and covered by smoke-clouds from the guns. . . . These puffs of smoke and [strange to say] the sound of the firing produced the chief beauty of the spectacle.

'Puff! puff!'—and two clouds arose pushing one another and blending together; and 'boom, boom!' came the sounds confirming what the eye had seen. . . . From the left, over fields and bushes, those large balls of smoke were continually appearing followed by their solemn reports, while nearer still, in the hollows and woods, there burst from the muskets small cloudlets that had no time to become balls, but had their little echoes in just the same way. 'Trakh—ta-ta-takh!' came the frequent crackle of musketry, but it was irregular and feeble in comparison with the reports of the cannon.*

This was before the battle began. This is how it was in full blast as seen from a redoubt in the centre of the Russian line.

By ten o'clock some twenty men had already been carried away from the battery, two guns were smashed and cannon-balls fell more and more frequently on the battery, and spent bullets buzzed and whistled around. . . . 'A live one!' shouted a man as a whistling shell approached. 'Not this way! To the infantry!' added another with loud laughter, seeing the shell fly past and fall into the ranks of the supports. 'Awkward baggage!' [cried a red-faced humorist] to a cannon-ball that struck a cannon-wheel and a man's leg.†

This description shows how similar battles were in 1812 to what

* Tolstoy, L., *War and Peace*, trans. Louise and Aylmer Maude. London, Macmillan, 1959, p. 873.
† Ibid., p. 878.

they have still remained. The range of activity was closer then and the cannon-balls moved more slowly and were, in consequence, more visible. And destructive though they were a century ago, they were less so than today. Here is the account of the battle as seen by a Russian officer.

Prince Andrew, pale and gloomy like everyone in the regiment, paced up and down. . . . There was nothing for him to do and no orders to be given. Everything went on of itself. The killed were dragged from the front, the wounded carried away, and the ranks closed up. 'Look out!' came a frightened cry from a soldier and, like a bird whirring in rapid flight and alighting on the ground, a shell dropped with little noise within two steps of Prince Andrew and close to the battalion commander's horse. The horse first, regardless of whether it was right or wrong to show fear, snorted, reared almost throwing the major, and galloped aside. . . . The smoking shell spun like a top. . . . At one and the same moment came the sound of an explosion, a whistle of splinters as from a breaking window-frame, a suffocating smell of powder, and Prince Andrew started to one side, raising his arm, and fell on his chest. Several officers ran up to him. From the right side of his abdomen blood was welling out making a large stain on the grass.*

Reading this vivid description 150 years later, we notice three differences from our own times: the low velocity of the shell, its ineffectiveness—Prince Andrew only died some weeks later from the scientific incompetence of the doctors of his day—and the horse.

The change in the efficiency of the artillery pieces was surprisingly slow. For the most part, Napoleon's cannons were made as cannons had been made for centuries before. That is to say, a hole was laboriously bored in a solid cylinder of iron. To use one of them, a bag of gunpowder and some wadding were stuffed in through the end of the muzzle and rammed down with a pole. The ball or shot was then put in on top and the gun was ready for firing. There were several disadvantages in this method of operation. Firstly, there was a limit to the force which the iron barrel could resist; consequently the amount of gunpowder, the size of the projectile and the distance which it could be fired were limited. Secondly, no way had been developed to introduce a spiral groove inside the barrel. This so-called rifling in modern weapons causes the projectile to spin and thus travel very much straighter through the air. Consequently, before this technological innovation was introduced, the accuracy with which artillery

* Ibid., p. 895.

35

pieces could be aimed was comparatively low. A third limitation was that gunpowder, a mixture of charcoal, sulphur and saltpetre, while possessing many advantages in warfare—for example, it is not particularly likely to explode accidentally—produced so much smoke that the gunners soon found themselves unable to see what they were doing. It also quickly fouled the barrels of the guns, which needed to be repeatedly cleaned if any reasonable degree of accuracy was to be maintained in the shooting. A final technical disadvantage which the men of the 1850s had to deal with was the recoil of the guns. The expanding gases of the burning gunpowder simultaneously push the shot forward and the gun back. Since the gun was firmly fixed to its carriage, the whole thing—gun and carriage—recoiled backwards every time the piece was fired and the men working it had to push it back into position again for reloading and re-aiming after every shot.

The revolution in guns, small arms, shells, tanks—in fact in the whole mechanics of war, like the technology of almost everything else—changed in two waves. The first, between the middle of the eighteenth and middle of the nineteenth century, coincides with what is sometimes called The First Industrial Revolution. During this period when the steam engine came into use and factories housing textile machinery grew up, the innovations introduced, although they were generally based on the scientific understanding of the times, did not depend on scientific research specifically aimed at industrial ends. The later part of the technological revolution, in which we continue to live today, is sometimes designated The Second Industrial Revolution. During this period, scientific studies were undertaken directly to meet practical needs. This division of the Industrial Revolution into two parts is not clear-cut nor is it entirely justifiable to fix a particular time when one method of approach was superseded by another. The change in the technology of gunnery, however, exemplified rather well the two kinds of advance.

First of all, improvements were introduced to make gun-barrels stronger so that shells could be fired farther. In the 1830s a French engineer, Thiery, devised a system for surrounding the cast-iron barrel with steel hoops which were shrunk on so as to bind the barrel tightly and prevent its bursting; this was further modified by an American, Daniel Treadwell, in 1841. A few years later, another American, a man called Rodwell, invented a system in which, instead of boring a solid barrel and then strengthening it with hoops, he cast the barrel round a central core and then cooled it in such a way that the outer layers, which were kept hot longer than the inner ones, shrank during cooling and thus exerted the same gripping effect as had the steel hoops. A few years later still, as the general march of technology advanced and steel became plentiful, it displaced cast-iron altogether and stronger and larger steel gun-barrels, with internal rifling grooves became general. Then in the 1860s and 1870s, simultaneously in France, Germany, Spain and America, the engineering problem of how to load guns from the breech end of the barrel instead of from the muzzle end was solved. Finally, towards the end of the nineteenth century, a way of suspending the barrel of a gun on a cradle and interposing a system of compression cylinders and heavy spiral springs between it and the fixed mounting was devised to allow the barrel only to recoil after the shot was fired and then return to its firing position. None of these advances was particularly 'scientific' although they were useful and important and were only achieved when the general level of knowledge and skill had advanced far enough to make them possible. They can be considered characteristic of The First Industrial Revolution.

The second kind of improvement in gunnery was very much more related to the advance in pure science—particularly the knowledge of chemistry—which gained momentum in the middle of the nineteenth century. Napoleon and the other generals who fought with him and against him had to depend on gunpowder both to propel their projectiles and explode such shells as they might use. Gunpowder cannot claim to have been a scientific discovery. Its action depends on the fact that the oxygen needed to bring about the combustion of the sulphur and the carbon of the charcoal is compounded within it as part of the saltpetre (potassium nitrate). When gunpowder is set alight this oxygen, intimately mixed with the carbon and sulphur, causes a rapid evolution of gas. The volume occupied by the original powder almost instantaneously becomes 4,000 times as big as it was before. The discovery of its action dates back to the medieval days of the thirteenth century. The saltpetre, which is its essential ingredient, is produced by the action of bacteria on putrefying nitrogenous organic matter. For example, the sewage-saturated soil around Indian villages has been a traditional source of 'nitre' for ages. In Sweden the peasants were compelled to maintain nitre-beds and in France the rights of collection were farmed for many years. It is interesting to recall that from medieval times right up to the time of Lavoisier at the end of the eighteenth century, the same unscientific source of saltpetre, the key munition of war, retained its monopoly. In fact, nitre-beds, after falling out of use in the middle of the nineteenth century, as I shall describe, were temporarily revived in the southern states of America as late as 1864.

As we have seen, gunpowder possesses its explosive properties because the oxygen locked in the molecule of saltpetre, KNO_3, is intimately mixed—just as one might mix face-powder—with charcoal and sulphur. In 1845 C. F. Schönbein succeeded in preparing a chemical compound possessing a structure in which the fuel atoms (C and H) are packed in the same molecule with the required oxygen atoms in the most intimate kind of association conceivable. Most of the oxidisable atoms are held away from the oxygen atoms by 'buffer atoms' of nitrogen; but the nitrogen–oxygen link is not a strong one and impulses provided by heat, shock or detonation are sufficient to upset the molecular equipoise and start off the explosion. This compound was guncotton—cellulose nitrate—made by treating cotton, which is almost pure cellulose, with nitric and sulphuric acids. At first, although the scientific acumen of Schönbein discovered it, it was so devastatingly dangerous to handle that no one was able to use it until the technological ability of Sir F. A. Abel was brought to bear by showing that if it were pulped, like rags are when used in paper-making, it became stable.

A similar example of technology coming to the rescue of science occurred with nitroglycerine. This also is an explosive molecule; it was prepared by Sobrero, professor of chemistry at Turin, in 1847. Nitroglycerine is an oily liquid. Drop a bottle of it and it will explode and kill you. It was so dangerous that nobody could safely use it until in 1867, after eight years' work during which his younger brother was killed in a terrible explosion, Alfred Nobel hit on the technological device of mixing the chemical compound, nitroglycerine, with the porous earth, kieselguhr. This mixture, which could now be handled without risking the lives of the people using it, was dynamite.

The history of the way in which science was suddenly embraced by the nations of the West is a remarkably uniform story. In medicine, metallurgy, the manufacture of goods of all sorts, and in warfare knowledge gradually accrued over a period of centuries. Even after the modern approach to science began in the seventeenth century

12: The Crimean War, 1855. Manhandling and muzzle-loading.   13: The gun-turret of H.M.S. *Majestic*, 1898. Scientific breech-mechanism.

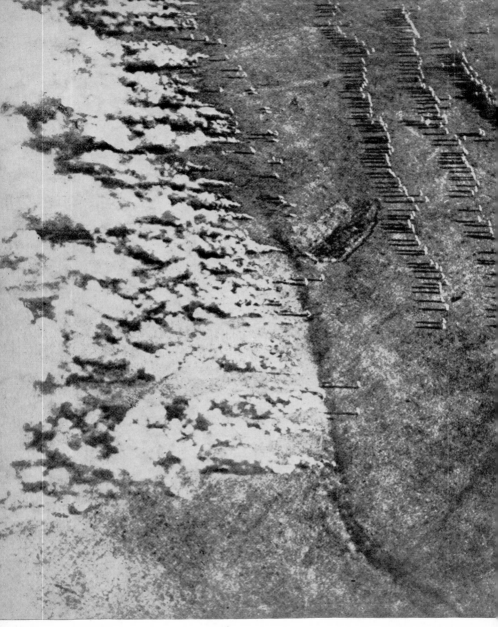

14: Chemical warfare between civilised nations. An aerial photograph of a gas attack taken above the Eastern Front, 1915.

15: Bikini Atoll, 1951—a milestone in human history. How seriously does mankind now take the word 'Bikini'? 16: A helicopter in Borneo. Hand-to-hand fighting persists into the scientific age.

17: The packet-boat of 1850 welcomed a fair wind just as the Phoenicians had. J. M. W. Turner, 'An English packet arriving' (*Tate Gallery, London*).   18: Paddington Station', by W. P. Frith, London, 1862 (*Royal Holloway College*).

there remained a gulf between natural philosophy—that is, scientific knowledge about Nature—and practical affairs. Scientists devoted themselves to unlocking the secrets of the universe. The social drive was to find things out. Then—and the change was abrupt—the urge changed. Starting with the steam engine as a model, men suddenly set themselves to apply ideas and the new knowledge of science to do practical things. And this is very much our intellectual attitude today. The main purpose in training men and women in science is not to discover the workings of Nature so much as to increase the wealth, comfort and power of the nation.

Gunpowder was used in war for 600 years. Then suddenly in the nineteenth century people began to think about the fundamental nature of its action: that is, they considered the scientific principles of the chemical reaction involved and their attitude changed. Instead of supposing that improvement would come from training gunpowder-makers better in their trade, they took thought on how they could better apply the principle of which a gunpowder explosion was one example. This is the modern scientific approach and it bore fruit as readily in the 1860s as in the 1960s.

Following the discovery of guncotton (and its modified version, cordite) and nitroglycerine and dynamite, there came in quick succession the so-called 'aromatic' nitro-compounds. The first was tri-nitro-phenol. Scientific knowledge of this compound, commonly called picric acid, had been in existence in 1771, but practical use for gunnery only came in 1885 when the more propitious intellectual climate had set in. In the Boer War in 1901, the British used cordite as a propellent and picric acid as a bursting charge in the propelled shells. The French and the Japanese did the same but the Germans used tri-nitro-toluene (TNT) as an improvement on tri-nitro-phenol. And so we come almost to the modern age.

Napoleon, like a Moses who was only permitted to look forward from the top of Mount Pisgah into the Promised Land but not to enter it, could see the flowering of science in France and in the other nations of Europe but did not himself survive as a political figure to lead his countrymen into the technological state. Even while his soldiers were blazing away with their muskets, using the sparks from their flints to ignite the gunpowder which propelled their bullets, the Reverend Alexander Forsyth had conceived the principle by which small-arms fire could be made vastly more accurate, convenient to operate, and lethal. Forsyth was a sporting Scottish clergyman; he was a well-educated man with a good knowledge of chemistry: in 1807 he patented the percussion cap.

To discharge a firearm, whether it were a great cannon or a portable hand gun, it had always been necessary to put a match to the touch-hole and set light to the gunpowder. This could be a clumsy operation and, for soldiers using muskets and fighting in the rain, might be uncertain as well. Numerous devices were elaborated during the slow pre-scientific evolution of military technique. For example, the touch-hole was moved from the top of the gun's circumference to the side so that the first drops of rain would not fall directly in and wet the powder. Instead of using a heated wire to fire the charge, a 'match' was devised made of hemp soaked in a solution of saltpetre which would smoulder without going out. Later still, the flint-lock was invented by which a shower of sparks was induced when the hammer fell on a flint. The revolutionary intellectual stride achieved by the Reverend Mr Forsyth was to use the newly discovered chemistry of his time; he enclosed a pinch of 'percussion powder'—largely potassium chlorate—in a tube the end of which was pushed into the powder of the charge. When the hammer of the piece was caused to fall it crushed the metal tube, the 'percussion powder' detonated and produced a flash which set off the gunpowder.

This device, a nice combination of science and technique, revolutionised the operations of musketry. While the technologists set to work to improve the arrangement of the percussion cap—by combining it with the cartridge; by redesigning the metal case in which the detonating charge was contained; by causing the hammer to fall, first on the edge of the cartridge (this was called 'rim-fire'); then on the centre of the cartridge; by redesigning the hammer, introducing devices for preventing gases from leaking backwards when the piece was discharged and elaborating first a pin and later on a shaped rim so that the spent cartridge could be withdrawn—while all this was going on, the chemists were at work too. It was not long before potassium chlorate was replaced as a detonator by a compound of more effective molecular configuration, the so-called 'fulminate of mercury'.

The historical changes brought about by scientific ideas in the art of war and in the behaviour of the men gathered together in armies to exercise this art show in a vivid yet paradoxical way the manner in which similar changes came about in society at large. A group of men organised as an army is in one respect particularly resistant to innovation and change. Yet at the same time the pressures of war and the intensity with which men live their lives under battle conditions—after all, as Dr Johnson put it, 'Depend upon it, Sir, when a man knows he is to be hanged in a fortnight, it concentrates his mind wonderfully'—accelerate the speed at which new ideas are tested. The resistance to change is aptly exemplified in an account given by Professor Elting Morison in a lecture published in 1958. It refers to that most persistent of military tools used from biblical wars up to the charge of the Lancers at Omdurman in which Winston Churchill took part as a young man: I refer to the horse.

In the early days of World War II after the retreat from Dunkirk in 1940, the British army were using every available gun to defend the south coast of England. Among these were some light artillery left over from the Boer War of 1901, which were dragged about by motor lorries. In order to get the most effective results out of these good but nevertheless somewhat old-fashioned guns, a time-and-motion study was instituted in order to find out how the most rapid rate of firing could be achieved. One of the efficiency experts studying a film of a gun's crew operating asked why it was that just before each discharge of the gun two members of the crew stood stiffly apart doing nothing. At last, a very old gunnery officer remembered that when the drill had originally been devised, these men's duty was to hold the horses.

Professor Morison has described a more important and interesting example showing in historical terms how a scientific innovation depends on two factors; first, knowledge and the ideas springing from it and, second, the will to introduce the innovation. His account is of 'continuous-aim firing' of naval guns at sea. Before this system was introduced in 1898, the naval gunner faced with the problem of firing at a target from the rolling deck of a ship at sea, would first reckon the range. He would raise his gun-barrel to the appropriate elevation to allow the shell to carry for the appropriate distance. Then he would look along the sights of the gun as the ship rolled and at the exact moment when the movement of the deck brought the sights in line with the target he would press the firing button. This method of operation possessed two principal disadvantages. Firstly, the rate of fire was very slow because the gun could only be discharged when the roll of the vessel allowed it to point at the proper elevation. The second weakness of the procedure was that no matter how quickly the gunner brought his hand down on the button there was bound to be some delay between the time when, with his eye on the sights, he had the impulse to fire and the moment when he had, in fact, converted the impulse into action. What in practice good gunners trained themselves to do was to try to guess how violently their ships were rolling and then press the button a short time before the sights of the gun pointed at the target.

In spite of the best efforts of the most skilful gun-aimers, the accuracy of naval gunfire before 1898 was deplorably bad. For example, during one particular exercise, five ships of the North Atlantic squadron fired for twenty-five minutes at a hulk set up as a target at a range of 1,600 yards and only scored two hits! Considering that the mathematical laws describing the trajectory of a cannon-ball had been worked out by Galileo at the end of the sixteenth century, this was a pathetic performance and illustrated how inadequately technique had kept pace with theoretical knowledge.

The solution to the problem was discovered by Admiral Sir Percy Scott, a quarrelsome and frustrated officer of the British Navy who, in 1898, was in command of H.M.S. *Scylla*. One rough day, when his crew were engaged in gunnery target practice and were, as might be expected, shooting particularly badly, he noticed that one gun-aimer consistently achieved a better score than any of the others. Admiral Scott watched the man carefully and noticed that his method of working the gun was to operate the elevating gear up and down in an attempt to compensate, at least partially, for the rolling of the ship. He instantly conceived the idea that in order to control the flight of the shell what was needed was, not to keep the gun still relative to the ship and only fire it at one particular (and, in fact, unattainable) instant, but on the contrary to keep the gun still relative to the target. Seized with this idea, he fitted a far more flexible elevating gear to the gun so that the gun-aimer, by moving the handles backwards and forwards in time with the motion of the ship, kept the sights of the gun constantly pointing at the target.

Six years after he had changed the system of gunnery in his ships by this early example of the principle of relativity, the improvement in the results obtained by his gunners was spectacular. In practice firing, at the same range and under the same conditions in which before twenty-five minutes of gunfire had produced two hits, one gunner scored fifteen hits in one minute, half of them on a bull's-eye 50 inches square.

The history of Admiral Percy Scott and his new scientific ideas about naval warfare is interesting in two respects. Firstly, it represents in a particularly 'pure' way, an example of the way in which an idea— an intellectual conception—can affect practical affairs. Scott's idea, that the gun should be kept 'still' while the ship on which it was mounted should be allowed to roll about underneath it, did not require elaborate hardware. To change the gear-ratio of the elevating mechanism was not very difficult. A further innovation introduced by Scott was the mounting of improved telescopic sights so that the aimer could keep his gun pointing accurately at the target, and this telescope was mounted on a slide in order to avoid what was previously a common accident, namely, the aimer being struck in the eye by the telescope when the gun recoiled. But the second interesting feature about continuous-aim firing was that, in spite of the spectacular successes demonstrated by its use, the British Admiralty, the United States Bureau of Ordnance and the United States Bureau of Navigation, far from welcoming the new system, strongly resisted its introduction.

The history of the last hundred years—the Science Century—while it is unique among all other centuries in the narrative of mankind for the avidity with which technological innovations, some based on existing knowledge and some developed from new scientific discoveries, have been embraced, can also show many examples of the stubbornness with which certain of these technological developments have been resisted. Although it is not easy to know why it was that only in the eighteenth century and more particularly in the nineteenth century did the educated communities of the West suddenly desire technological advance, it can be seen as reasonable that once this desire had become generally accepted, resistance to the main trend, where it appeared, should be quickly swept away.

In due course, as the nineteenth century gave place to the twentieth and the tide of scientific philosophy as the main motive of human behaviour rose, the sand-castle of opposition was swept away. In the final development of the battleship, the principle of continuous-aim firing, conceived in 1898, has been developed by the application of a variety of scientific and technological refinements. The greatly increased range of the guns, making it impossible for the gun-aimer to keep them pointed at the target by 'eyeball sighting', necessitated the introduction of radar. No new principle was, however, evolved in arranging appropriate machinery to keep the gun-barrels pointing at the target mechanically instead of by manually operated handles. Allowance was made for the wind speed (recorded by an appropriate anemometer), for the variation in air-resistance (calculated from records of temperature and humidity and barometric pressure), and for the known speed of the ship and the estimated speed of the target. All these types of measurement ('parameters' as they are called in the jargon of science) can readily be integrated by a computer in the ship's control tower so that the guns are made to swing up and down relative to the motion of the ship or, if one looks at the matter differently, can be kept motionlessly directed towards the target as the ship moves relatively to the gun turret, in exactly the way envisaged by Admiral Percy Scott.

So far we have only considered in the main one aspect of the way in which the advance of scientific understanding and its technical application to practical affairs have affected warfare in the hundred years between the mid-1800s and the mid-1900s. This has been the use of chemistry in devising more powerful propellents and more destructive missiles to propel. These advances in technology have been paralleled by improvements in the construction of guns of all sorts, making them capable of being loaded and discharged more rapidly and, as we have just discussed, aimed more accurately. But two other general advances besides the introduction of chemical science into warfare have been the improvement in communications and the acceleration of movement. It is, however, not necessary to discuss these separately in a consideration of warfare. The disappearance of the horse as the fastest means of transporting both men and messages produced effects as fundamental to the society of communities at peace as to those at war and will be considered at length later. Similarly, the improvement in communications, from the semaphore telegraph—in which, as it happens, Napoleon was greatly interested; indeed, he organised the setting up of 'trunk lines' of high towers equipped with an arrangement of movable arms by which messages could be transmitted right across France by men seated on the towers with telescopes to their eyes—to the heliograph of the Boer War of 1901 by which a mirror flashing the light of the sun was used to send information by means of a code introduced by the American inventor of the electric telegraph, Samuel Morse, in 1844, all the way to the clumsy and unreliable wire-conveyed systems of the 1914–18 war and thence to the far more sophisticated radio communications of World War II and twenty years beyond—all this deserves, like transport, a chapter to itself.

*   *   *

Each of the steps by which the century's rapid advance in scientific knowledge was applied to the technology of military affairs is interesting and remarkable of itself. The disappearance of gunpowder after 600 years' use and the subsequent eclipse of the horse after an even longer period both represented technological revolutions. The improvement in the precision and force of firearms made it necessary to change the basis of military tactics. Whereas before a massed group of men formed a strong unit for both attack and defence, this method of operation surviving from Roman armies of classical times could no longer be used. At the Battle of Waterloo in 1815, a solid 'square' of infantry armed with muskets could usefully be opposed to charging cavalry. In 1901, however, in South Africa, when professional artillerymen, behaving as they had been trained to do, formed up their guns in solid lines to bombard concealed Boer farmers armed with what were then modern German precision rifles, they and their horses were destroyed by withering fire. Later still, in World War I, when massed infantry were ordered to leave the trenches in which they were sheltering below ground level and advance against opponents armed with machine guns, it was again demonstrated that accurate fire, with an intensity now multiplied by automatic weapons, could not be resisted in so archaic a manner.

Warfare at sea, like that on land, has undergone the same abrupt changes during the last hundred years. After a thousand years or more of wooden ships moved by the wind, the Industrial Revolution brought iron ships driven by steam. A few iron ships appeared as early as 1780 but not until the 1830s did they begin to be accepted. This delay was due to the remarkable intellectual 'block' in otherwise rational minds at the notion that an iron vessel would float, although common experience with a bucket must have demonstrated that it did and Archimedes' principle, known to scholars since 250 B.C., enabled the buoyancy of any particular design to be calculated.

Iron ships driven by steam were stronger and could move more swiftly and with greater freedom than wooden ones propelled by sails. Such modifications certainly changed the character of naval warfare. But the main difference brought about in the hundred years from 1850 to 1950 were—as on land—the longer range and more accurate aim of artillery; and the fighting man at sea has to deal with explosive missiles projected through the water in the form of torpedoes as well as those shot through the air as shells. As part of this change, there was the introduction of radar in World War II, at the end of the historical period we are considering, indeed almost where modern history becomes the present time. This entirely scientific innovation allowed guns to be aimed at night and ships at sea (or in the air) to be 'seen'—and hit—when out of sight. Although the discovery of radar has indeed been of peculiar significance to the conduct of naval warfare in our own times, its more fundamental philosophical implications are worth a moment's consideration.

Human consciousness until the end of the nineteenth century was dependent on the five senses: smell, taste, touch, hearing and sight. With these cut off, man as a human being, regardless of whether his cells and tissues continue to live or not, ceases to exist. Scientific devices have, since the earliest days of science, extended the powers of the senses. The telescope and the microscope greatly increase the ability to see, and later, such devices as the telegraph and the telephone, and the invention of printing as well, enhanced human powers of hearing and learning of the events going on in the world around. But these technological developments only extend, even if to a very great degree, man's existing senses. A modern citizen hears the voice of a speaker either direct or through a telephone and the sound is brought to his ear and hence to his brain by vibrations of the air. The structure of an insect's wing or the moons of the planet Saturn are brought to the consciousness of an entomologist or an astronomer by the photons of light which stimulate the nerve-endings of the retina of his eye. But pre-scientific man, just like the modern man of science, has always heard sound waves of air and has always seen photons of light. In perceiving by radar a ship through the dense darkness of a foggy night when it is—if language is to retain its meaning—out of sight, neither sound waves, nor light rays, nor for that matter warmth nor smell, play any part.

In 1887, it was shown by the German physicist, Heinrich Hertz, that radiated electromagnetic waves are reflected from solid objects. This discovery in theoretical science was first put to use in a technological device by Christian Hulsmeyer in 1904. Hulsmeyer's idea was to discharge an electromagnetic wave and record any echo which might come back should the wave strike a solid object. The device— remarkably up-to-date in its day—was to prevent collisions at sea. Marconi described the principle involved in a speech which he gave in 1922 and two Americans, Breit and Tuve, elaborated a device at the Carnegie Institute of Washington by which electromagnetic pulses were reflected back from the ionosphere, one of the layers of ionised gas by which the earth is encased.

The principle of 'radio detection and ranging'—radar, for short— was first used seriously (and with outstanding success) in war in 1940 when a chain of towers built round the coast of England and equipped with apparatus designed by the Scottish physicist, Sir Robert Watson-Watt, at the National Physical Laboratory, sent out pulses of radiation which, reflected back from the bomber squadrons of the Luftwaffe, enabled the much smaller force of British fighter aircraft to track their course, 'see' them while they were still out of sight and attack them when they arrived.

The new science-derived process of 'seeing' by means of a new agent, radio waves, undetectable by the senses, has been developed to a highly sophisticated degree. The savage hears a noise and knows that another man has called; a civilised man uses the same kind of ears and the same sound waves but, by means of a learned language, can by making noises discuss the philosophical basis of behaviour and the history of the bi-metallic system in the economic growth of China. The early 'bleep' on a radar screen was soon succeeded by the IFF system, whereby the radar pulse elicited a response identifying the echo as having emanated from a friend or a foe. But radio waves as a signal additional to light, sound, touch, smell and feeling have shown mankind much more than this. They have brought information about the universe, and this is of a different order of significance than squalid details of human war.

In 1931, Karl Jansky, an American engineer working in the laboratories of the Bell Telephone Company, had the quick-wittedness to notice that his ultra-short-wave radio set made a howling noise at regular intervals of exactly 23 hours and 56 minutes. He deduced from this that the beam of radio waves his set was receiving came from outer space and was picked up each time the earth revolved to bring him back to the receiving point. It is now clear that besides the stars we know about from the light they emit, there are others in the firmament which we cannot see but which make their existence known by the radio waves they send out. Science, in fact, has provided us with a new sense by which to understand the universe. This ability we owe to progress in natural philosophy and also to the historical development of devices for war.

As I have pointed out, each of the small particular advances in military science has been interesting and some have been important. But the cumulative effects of the two trends have been of major historical significance.

From the time of Napoleon to that of Kaiser William II, fighting was a profession carried on by soldiers and sailors. Citizens who did not belong to this profession were only incidentally concerned with wars. The advances in technology which have changed this are, firstly, the improvement in the efficiency of weapons allowing them to be reloaded and fired more and more quickly, and the increase in artillery range. As long as cannons had to be swabbed out between each shot and then laboriously reloaded from the muzzle end and re-aimed, artillerymen could be kept supplied comparatively easily. By World War I, however, things were found—to the surprise of the generals—to have changed. When the war started, the British calculated that the probable expenditure of shot by their guns would amount to seven rounds of the biggest pieces of field artillery per day. This estimate, like that of the French and the German commanders, was far too low. It was found, when the battle was joined, that 500 rounds a day or more were needed. To supply this and all the other munitions required by the burgeoning technology, for machine guns and other automatic weapons and much else, the industry of the whole nation had to be committed to the task. The civil population could no longer remain neutral while the armies fought. Entire communities were drawn into the supply departments; nations found themselves in truth committed to war. It was no longer a matter just of armies.

The technical achievement of the long-range artillery has in the last two generations of modern history drawn every citizen into the firing lines as well as into the lines of supply. Napoleon's guns could cast a shell less than 2,000 yards. At the start of World War I, the advance in chemical science provided propellents capable of pro-jecting a missile to a range of more than 10,000 yards. In the early years of World War II, shells could be fired the 22 miles—39,000 yards—across the English Channel. And by October the 4th, 1957, the limit had been reached.

The use of aircraft to drop bombs represented a simple extension of technology applied to gunnery. In a battle—in any battle from the Middle Ages to the present day—the operation of shooting things at the enemy falls into two parts. Tactical fire may take the form of throwing a spear at a man standing in front of you, or letting off a tommy gun. Strategic fire can be the casting of heavy shot with a catapult to destroy the enemy's quarters while the men in front maintain a rapid hail of arrows, or it can be a barrage of shells from heavy howitzers in the rear of a modern entrenched army. Alterna-tively, the strafing of troops by aircraft can be used in place of tactical gunfire while the bombing of their home cities is merely an extension of the role of heavy guns. By the end of World War II, aircraft and artillery had become indistinguishable. The German V1-rocket possessed vestigial wings and a motor and was a flying bomb. The Japanese Kamikadze suicide planes were flying bombs too. Finally, technology, aided by chemical science to design the fuel and mathe-matics and physics to work out the trajectory, produced the V2-rocket capable of travelling 200 miles. And the war ended.

Then, on October the 4th, 1957, the Russians fired a rocket part of which did not land at all. This was Sputnik 1: the sign that the history of war technology had reached its last phase. From that date, war, like peace, could be seen to be indivisible.

With the development of rockets capable of putting a projectile into orbit—quite apart from aircraft travelling faster than the speed of sound—no part of the earth was out of range of an enemy situated on any other part of the earth. And the projectile is no longer a mere explosive shell, it is a nuclear bomb. Einstein in 1905, by taking thought, conceived the idea that mass—the material stuff of the nucleus of elemental matter—was in truth the incarnation of pro-digious energy. In 1930, Otto Hahn and Lise Meitner discovered that the nucleus of an atom of uranium could be made to split and release energy in the vast proportion which Einstein had foreseen from his theoretical calculations. Then, on July the 16th, 1945, in the Alamo-gordo desert in America the modern chapter of military history began and an atomic bomb was exploded with a force equivalent to 20,000 tons of TNT. Three weeks later, on August the 6th, 1945, the populous city of Hiroshima was destroyed by a bomb of just this size.

Quickly the science century rolled on. In April 1948 an American nuclear explosion equal to 48,000 tons of TNT was let off. The following year a Russian bomb with the power of 50,000 tons of TNT exploded. Five years later this was followed by the explosion of a so-called hydrogen bomb with the force of 1 million tons of TNT. Within six months, on March the 1st, 1954, an American thermonuclear bomb equivalent to the bursting of 15 million tons of TNT was loosed near the Pacific island of Bikini. For the Russians to explode a bomb of 20 million tons of TNT-equivalence in October 1957 was almost an irrelevance. The age of military power of limitless destructiveness had clearly arrived.

The growth of power of such awful magnitude has had an interesting and rather unexpected effect on modern military history. To prevent the other side delivering their bombs, industrialised nations set their scientists to work to develop sophisticated electronic systems to guide artillery shells and rockets so that they would 'home' on to any target at which they were aimed. The effect of this was to make it impossible for a potential enemy to operate a large piloted bombing aircraft or a large, expensive aircraft carrier at sea within range of the new artillery. Consequently, battleships, after having become bigger and bigger, more powerful and more heavily armed were seen to have begun to become vulnerable and useless. And so it was with the big bombers. The infinitely destructive nuclear rockets were, therefore, either buried far away in deep bunkers or hidden under the sea in submarines, themselves powered with nuclear engines to free them from the necessity of coming to shore—and in range of the opposition—to take on fuel. And because the nuclear weapons could be seen to be capable of destroying friend and foe alike, the new wars—in Korea, in Indo-China, in Algeria, Borneo and Central Africa—began to resemble the old ones about which Tolstoy wrote. To be sure, the soldiers fighting them could be carried about in helicopters and equipped with repeating rifles and recoil-less guns projecting rocket shells. Yet for the men, wet, tired, frightened, carrying heavy loads through unfamiliar forests, the rigours and savagery of war were little changed.

CHAPTER IV

THE TRAIN, THE AUTOMOBILE,
THE AIRCRAFT—AND THE BICYCLE

On August the 18th, 1773, having left Edinburgh in the morning and crossed the Firth of Forth by boat, about 5 miles below the place where the road bridge now stands, Dr Johnson and Boswell arrived at Kinghorn in the county of Fife. This is a journey which today would occupy about half an hour. 'We dined at Kinghorn,' wrote Boswell in his diary, 'and then got into a post-chaise. Mr Nairne and his servant, and Joseph, rode by us. We stopped at Cupar, and drank tea. We talked of parliament; and I said, I supposed very few of the members knew much of what was going on.' The distance from Kinghorn to Cupar is 18 miles. 'We had a dreary drive,' Boswell went on, 'in a dusky night, to St Andrews, where we arrived late.' From Cupar to St Andrews is 10 miles.

A little later in the holiday, on August the 30th when they had reached Inverness, Boswell continued,

> This day we were to begin our *equitation*. We might have taken a chaise to Fort Augustus but, had we not hired horses at Inverness, we should not have found them afterwards: so we resolved to begin here to ride. We had three horses, for Dr Johnson, myself and Joseph, and one which carried our portmanteaus, and two Highlanders who walked along with us.*

This, then, was travelling in 1773. Civilised conversation, ideas about parliament very like our own, but travel in a chaise at 8 m.p.h. or thereabouts and, on less frequented roads, on horseback at a walking-pace with the luggage on a pack-horse. The good conversation and the civilised ideas equalling or excelling our own but the technological revolution in travel still to come. And the lack of change which had subsisted since the Romans—indeed there had been a regression in the state of the roads since the Romans—was to continue for almost another century. More than sixty years after

* Boswell, J., *The Journal of a Tour in the Hebrides with Samuel Johnson, LL.D.* London, Nelson, 1785.

Johnson and Boswell took their journey round Scotland, Charles Dickens—jeering at the whole idea of science in reporting on the resolution unanimously agreed by the Pickwick Club, 'That this Association has heard read, with feelings of unmingled satisfaction and unqualified approval the paper communicated by Samuel Pickwick, Esq., G.C.M.P.C., entitled "Speculations on the source of the Hampstead Ponds, with some observations on the Theory of Tittlebats" '—quoted Mr Pickwick as saying 'he could not but feel that they had selected him for a service of great honour, and of some danger. Travelling was in a troubled state, and the minds of coachmen were unsettled. Let them look abroad and contemplate the scenes which were enacting around them. Stage-coaches were upsetting in all directions, horses were bolting, boats were overturning and boilers were bursting. . . .'

Dickens wrote this in 1837. Travellers then moved about the country, wrapped in greatcoats, in unheated stage-coaches, stifling inside or chilled to the bone and often soaking wet from the rain outside on the roof. Each time the horses were changed, the passengers could, if they wished, warm and refresh themselves by drinking the variety of hot alcoholic beverages which the pages of Dickens describe. But this was the end of an era, and it is interesting to consider how sharp was the boundary between the historical period it described and the next.

In 1837, when the *Pickwick Papers* came out, the scientific ideas of the great Newton and his peers, Galileo and Kepler, were part of scholarship. The understanding of chemistry, that is the ideas of Priestley and Lavoisier and their contemporaries, had followed the earlier discoveries in physics. And in technology, that is the *application* of scientific knowledge, much had already happened. The Newcomen steam engine came into use for pumping water out of coal-mines as early as 1712 when a machine was installed at Dudley Castle in Staffordshire. Very much improved steam plant was common by the end of the century. Mr Pickwick, it will be recalled, describes later on the industrialisation of Birmingham when he travelled—still by horse-drawn carriage—with Mr Bob Sawyer, Sam Weller and the bibulous Mr Benjamin Allen on the dickey behind, to call on Mr Winkle's father.

As they rattled through the narrow thoroughfares leading to the heart of the turmoil, the sights and sounds of earnest occupation struck more forcibly on the senses. The streets were thronged with working-people. The hum of labour resounded from every house, lights gleamed from the long casement windows in the attick stories, and the whirl of wheels and noise of machinery shook the trembling walls. The fires, whose livid, sullen light had been visible for miles blazed fiercely up in the great works and factories of the town. The din of hammers, the rushing of steam, and the dead heavy clanking of the engines, was the harsh music which arose from every quarter.*

Yet Mr Pickwick and his companions passed through this epitome of the technology of the First Industrial Revolution behind a horse, briskly driven by a postboy. Six years later, when Robert Surtees brought out *Handley Cross*, the pregnant change was becoming apparent. Mr John Jorrocks, the comic grocer who accepted the invitation to assume the mastership of the Handley Cross foxhounds, travelled down from London to assume the dignity of M.F.H.-ship by train. And with him in the train, besides Mrs Jorrocks, his niece, his maid Batsay and his servant Binjamin, he also brought his two horses Xerxes and Arter-Xerxes and, on a flat car coupled behind, his carriage.†

Here in more detail is the nice mixture of scientific insight and technical ability by means of which James Watt made the steam engine work and the steam locomotive possible. Watt observed that there appeared to be a serious imbalance between the amount of heat which was needed to expand the steam required to *push* one side of the piston, compared with the amount of heat which needed to be extracted in condensing the steam into water on the other side of the piston in order to form the vacuum to *pull* the other side of the piston and hence make the engine work efficiently. Being a good scientist, as well as an exceptional technical man, Watt carried out a series of experiments to determine exactly *how much* heat there was in a given amount of steam and found that it was approximately six times as much as that present in the same weight of water at the same temperature. This showed him the problem he had to solve in condensing steam to produce his vacuum. 'Being struck with this remarkable fact,' he wrote, 'and not understanding the reason for it, I mentioned it to my friend Dr Black, who then explained to me his doctrine of latent heat, which he had taught for some time before

* Dickens, Charles, *Pickwick Papers*. London, Nelson Classics, p. 744.
† Surtees, R., *Handley Cross*. London, 1854, p. 114.

this period (the summer of 1764); but having myself been occupied with the pursuits of business, if I had heard of it, I had not attached importance to it, when I thus stumbled upon one of the material facts by which that beautiful theory is supported.'*

It can be seen from this—and a number of other instances could be adduced—that it is a mistake to imagine that Watt's steam engine was a mere technical device. True, Watt was a gifted engineer, but combined with his mechanical ingenuity, he also possessed scientific insight into the principles governing the forces and materials with which he was dealing.

Now let us observe how the same mingling of scientific understanding and technical ability was needed before railway trains drawn by steam locomotives came into existence.

There was very little science in the invention of iron railway-lines. It was, indeed, little more than an accident arising from the fact that in 1767 the market for iron in Great Britain was slack. To deal with what today we should call 'over-production', the proprietors of Coalbrookedale iron-works in Shropshire used up some long iron bars to overlay the wooden rails on which trucks used in the works were run. It was soon recognised that greater weights could be pulled by horses—or men—when the trucks were thus run on iron rails. But although it was seen equally clearly that the newly developed steam engine promised to provide unrivalled power for pulling trains of trucks about, the direct bull-at-a-gate, 'practical man's' approach to the problem of building a steam locomotive without first studying the principles involved was in the main unsuccessful.

William Murdock, while an employee of Messrs Boulton and Watt, built a workable 'steam carriage'. Richard Trevithick drove a 'steam coach', with seven or eight passengers aboard, up the hill from Weith to Camborne on Christmas Eve, 1801. In 1803, he built a 'tram engine' which pulled five trucks carrying 10 tons of iron and seventy people from Pennydurran to Cardiff on iron rails. Later still, in 1808, one of his locomotives attained a speed of 20 m.p.h.

But full success had to await the proper solution to a number of basic scientific problems. For example, in 1810 nobody knew the principles governing the friction exerted by the locomotive wheels on the iron rails. It was asserted—but without evidence—that smooth

* Quoted by J. B. Hart, *James Watt and the History of Steam Power*. London, Collins, 1961.

19: Mass-production in 1915. The Ford Motor Company looses the flood.   20: A motor-car is a private tool which has not yet been adapted for social use.

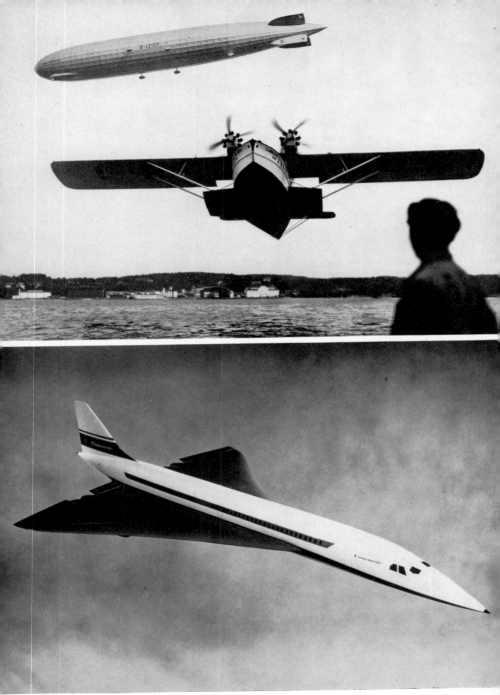

21: A Zeppelin of 1929, designed as an air ship; and a flying boat, designed as an air boat. Both now obsolete.   22. The Concorde supersonic aircraft. Its technical qualities and accompanying bangs have yet to be fitted into civilised life.

wheels would not pull a train along a smooth track and elaborate systems of cog-wheels engaging in a cogged track were devised. George Stephenson, the man who tackled the problems fundamentally, had little formal education but, like Priestley and Dalton and other great amateur scientists of the eighteenth century, he studied the principles of the phenomena with which he was dealing.

Stephenson's success was not an accident. He spent years studying different aspects of the problem. Besides fundamental investigations of the relationship between friction and the weight of a locomotive running on smooth rails, he demonstrated the superiority of wrought-iron over cast-iron for wheels and made substantial contributions towards perfecting the shape of wheels and their connection with the rails on which they were designed to run. His apotheosis came on September the 27th, 1825, when before a large crowd the Stockton to Darlington Railway—covering just eleven miles of the County of Durham—was ceremonially opened and the steam locomotive 'Active' drew a train of six waggons loaded with coals and flour, a passenger coach filled with the company directors and their friends, twenty-one waggons fitted with temporary seats and carrying nearly 450 passengers, and finally six waggon-loads of coal. The journey was successfully completed in sixty-five minutes. It was a major milestone in history.

The immediate revolution, resulting from the science of Boyle, whose 'law' related the volume of a gas to its temperature, and of Joseph Black and his elucidation of the principle of 'latent heat' and the technology of Newcomen and Watt and Stephenson and many others, was dramatic and, in some respects, painful. The opponents of change, the horse-breeders, canal owners and those concerned to preserve the large investment in roads and turnpikes fought a bitter battle. A century later, we can look back with mixed feelings as we recall Sir Isaac Coffin's speech in the House of Commons in which, after referring to these economic effects of the newly projected Liverpool and Manchester line, he said: 'It will be the greatest nuisance, the most complete disturbance of quiet and comfort in all parts of the kingdom, that the ingenuity of man could invent!'

This revolution could do nothing but succeed. In September 1830 the railway between Manchester and Liverpool was opened. Almost immediately the price of coal fell as its market increased, the price of land near the railway rose as it came within reasonable travelling-time of the great cities, and all economic activity was stimulated. The social goal of a nation in the nineteenth as in the twentieth century is—given the opportunity of choice—for economic expansion, not for quiet and comfort.

The first public railway was, as I have described, opened in 1825. In the 'thirties and 'forties other short local lines, laid down first of all in coal-mining districts, were developed into a national system for the whole of Great Britain. In 1839, the first edition of *Bradshaw's Railway Time Table* was issued by an enterprising Quaker desirous of being a help to mankind. In the 1840s a period of wild speculation broke out, the so-called 'railway mania' when everybody with money to invest, from rich gentlefolk to footmen, rushed to buy railway shares. Many of the investors lost their money but, just the same, the railway system of the country came into being. By 1843, 2,000 miles of railway had been built; five years later there was 5,000 miles of it. Heavy goods were transported by rail and the canals were bankrupted. Main roads fell into disuse, posting inns and postillions disappeared, the public mail-coaches no longer ran. But although long journeys were no more made by road, horse-traffic prospered for shorter journeys between one village and the next, from people's houses to the railway stations and within the towns made larger and busier because of the railways.

In 1848, Britain produced about half the pig-iron of the world; in the next thirty years the output trebled. Iron was needed for the railways themselves, for shipbuilding and for manufacture vastly increased by the improved transport facilities and by the full realisation of the importance to industrial productivity of steam power. The wealth of the country increased throughout the whole of society. In parallel with the great fortunes of the owners of industry, the real wages of a large proportion of the working people increased as well.

The achievement of British science and technology, combined with the drive to apply and develop, epitomised by George Stephenson, gave Britain at this time a remarkable supremacy. The first steam locomotives in European countries all came from England. The track-gauge of Stephenson's engines, which was merely the gauge of British mail-coaches, was adopted by most European countries. When the Nürnberg and Fürth Railway was opened on December the 7th, 1835, not only was the locomotive imported from England but the engine-driver, a Mr Wilson, was imported as well and he was paid a yearly wage of £225, illustrating the importance of the new 'aristocracy' of labour.

How dignified and proud he looked as he stood at the controls in his top hat. The *Stuttgarter Morgenblatt* described the occasion thus and sensed correctly that it was a historical turning-point.

> . . . the calm, deliberate behaviour of the engine-driver inspired confidence. Who could fail to see in such a man the personification of the whole difference between modern times and ancient or medieval days. Every shovelful of coal which he put in the furnace was added with careful thought for the correct quantity, the right moment, and the proper distribution. Not for a moment idle, keeping an eye on everything, calculating the minute at which he had to set the train in motion, he appeared like the ruling spirit of the machine and the elements united in it to develop enormous power. (December the 7th, 1835)

As in Britain, so in the rest of Europe and then throughout the world, railways sprang up as the outward and visible sign of the new technological thinking. By 1846 there were twenty-one railway companies in France—of which, subsequently, nineteen went bankrupt before the State took over the rest. Railways began to change the world. Countries and cities previously divided became linked. In 1841 an Austrian, Karl von Ghega, set out to build a line between Vienna, the land-locked centre of the Austro-Hungarian Empire, and the great and ancient port of Trieste. Apart from the technical and scientific problems involved—and von Ghega, boldly accepting the conclusions of theory, used smooth wheels and smooth rails even in the mountains—this was a major adventure of the human spirit. Doctors warned von Ghega that his passengers could never survive the journey over the Semmering Pass, reactionaries sabotaged his operations as the work of the Devil; a cholera epidemic caused the death of a thousand or more workmen. The mountains had to be blasted, tunnels dug, two-storey viaducts constructed. But in 1854 the Semmering Railway was built.

On the American continent, a British-built locomotive, 'The Stourbridge Lion', made one trip between two coal-mining towns, Carbondale and Hemesdale in Pennsylvania, in 1829, but the track was found not to be sufficiently strongly built and it was the following year, on Christmas Day, 1830, that the first locomotive, built in New York and brought to Charleston by sea, pulled a train in America. From that date, the growth of railways in the New World was as spectacular as in the Old and exercised as profound an effect on society. At last, in 1869, a railway journey could be made from the Atlantic to the Pacific when the Union Pacific Railway line from the Missouri River at Omaha, Nebraska, joined the Central Pacific Line from Sacramento, California, at Promontory in the State of Utah. Here then was a route, 1,776 miles in length, along which by the technology of the age communications could be maintained between the two separated sides of a continent and an individualistic collection of colonial settlements be knit together into a nation.

The steam locomotive has undoubtedly played a dominant part in the historical development of society during the past century. It is not, however, very easy to assess to what extent science, as such, was directly responsible for its advent. Clearly, a locomotive could only have become possible to a community in which scientific principles were understood, technological skills available, and where some people at least felt the urge to do new technical things. Although a number of men can be identified as being primarily responsible for the eventual production of a workable steam locomotive—Newcomen, Watt, Trevithick and others—and although the contributions of certain individual scientists provided essential knowledge towards the solution of the problems to be solved, the final emergence of the engine as a working machine was in many respects a process of stumbling evolution rather than the result of pure intellectual ratiocination.

No one scientist can ever be said to have succeeded alone, but in each age a single individual often stands out above his fellows. James Watt can, therefore, be accepted as a man whose work had a predominant influence on the history of the nineteenth century. He it was, above all others, who succeeded in amalgamating the confusing mixture of science, technical ideas, practical effectiveness and sheer drive which, with an appropriate seasoning of luck, are the ways in which major new advances so often come about. It is of great historical interest to contrast this blurred picture of the way the steam locomotive came into being and the effect which it exercised on its times with the story of Rudolf Diesel, almost a century later.

Diesel was a curious figure. He was a proud man, with a fanatical belief in the power of pure reason, a neurotic who suffered from chronic headaches and occasional breakdowns, a driven man with a mission to do for the twentieth century what James Watt had done for the nineteenth. His engine has, in fact, been responsible for the transformation of major sections of modern industry apart from its significance in ship propulsion and rail transport. But its particular historical interest is that it is a rare example of the way science is supposed to be applied to engineering—but almost never is. Diesel refused to accept that discoveries and innovations are most often mixtures of luck and empirical trial and error with a larding of science and forethought. The Diesel engine began as a pure idea.

When Rudolf Diesel was a student in 1879 he learned, during the course of a lecture given by Carl von Linde, that a steam engine only converted 6 to 10 per cent of the available heat of the fuel fed into it into effective work. This struck him as an affront to the dignity of the human intellect. For fourteen years he devoted his mind to the principles by which this state of affairs could be improved and in 1893 he published a book in which he set out the abstract theory of a 'rational heat engine', as he called it. And this work was issued before he had any hardware at all to back it up.

Diesel, although he succeeded in selling his pure idea to manufacturers for a handsome fortune—which was dissipated long before a commercially viable engine was produced by the Augsburg-Nürnberg Engine Works, reinforced later by Krupps of Essen—soon became greatly troubled because the engine did not turn out to be what he had said it was. The heavy, stationary design of the first motors was reduced in weight by Hugo Junkers so that, besides being a prime mover in a factory, the Diesel engine could also be used to drive locomotives, omnibuses and ships. Diesel's theoretical idea had been found to be sound: that heavy fuel oil could be sprayed into a cylinder and ignited directly by pressure and that the need to use fuel to convert water to steam before it could be made to produce power—that is, the inefficient 'steam cycle'—was unnecessary. But even though he had succeeded in demonstrating the supremacy of the scientific intellect, Diesel was not content. Tangled in a net of company flotation, patent litigation and business competition, and frustrated by the intransigence of real-life mechanics, he undertook an even more ambitious task: to reconstruct society on rational principles just as he had remodelled engines. He wrote down the principles by which this too should be done in his book, *Solidarismus*. But this time he could find no one to implement his ideas.

There is another small but significant technological wave in the advancing tide of human mobility that deserves mention. A savage, confronted by a modern bicycle, could not fail to see it as a marvel of applied science. The frame, of light, high-quality steel tubing wrought to a precise chemical analysis is quite beyond the range of any but a society of high technological expertise. The chromium-plated handlebars represent a further extension of esoteric skill and ability. The rubber of the pedals, indestructible, springy, derived from the up-to-date chemical knowledge of synthetic organic molecules, hardened by 'tumbling' in a freezing trough of solid carbon dioxide, is a further example of modern understanding and progress. The ball-bearings, the paint and enamel, the plastic saddle-bag, the glass bulb surrounding the filament of the lamp, the dynamo by which the lamp is lit—all these are far beyond the reach of the non-scientific citizen of only a century ago, whether he be as able as Newton or Socrates, Napoleon or Leonardo da Vinci. The development of the bicycle, however, was, like the steam locomotive, a mixture of non-science and science, forethought and accident. Nevertheless, its appearance and growth unquestionably had an influence on history.

The bicycle first appeared in something like a recognisable form in 1840 in Scotland when Kirkpatric MacMillan of Dumfries modified an eighteenth-century wheeled device, the dandy-horse, added cranks, driving rods and pedals and produced a 'velocipede'. In 1846 another Scot, Gavin Dalzell, improved the design and manufacture began. It is curious that these early machines were propelled by levers which had to be pumped up and down. The very much simpler and more direct method of pushing pedals round and round was only introduced after another twenty years, in 1865, by a workman employed by a French manufacturer, M. Michaux, in Paris. There was nothing scientific in this. The Michaux bicycles, with a heavy wooden frame and heavy wooden wheels fitted with iron tyres, became known as 'boneshakers'.

Next came 'penny-farthing ordinaries', with the front driving wheel, to which the pedals were fixed, made very large so that for each revolution of the wheel the bicycle would go farther. But when, in 1876, the 'safety' bicycle was invented, with the rear wheel driven, as at present, through a chain and sprocket, the dangerous penny-farthings became obsolete.

In the last quarter of the nineteenth century the bicycle was the fastest vehicle on the road. Cycling clubs sprang up in most of the countries of Europe and in America. The rustic countryside, cut off and forgotten by the advent of railways and the ruin of the stage-coach, was rediscovered. The cyclists brought pressure to bear on the authorities to improve the country roads. They improved country inns and lodging houses by approving of those which reached a satisfactory standard and passing over those that did not. By the 'nineties the bicycle—a technological, even if not quite a scientific product—played a hand in the emancipation of women. 'Safety' bicycles were well suited to ladies and they joined with men in touring through the countryside or went on trips by themselves. And since the long skirts of Victorian times were inconvenient on a bicycle, the freedom of the road led to a parallel advance in freedom of dress. Not every lady was in sympathy with the formidable American dress-reformer and advocate of women's rights, Mrs Amelia Jenks Bloomer, who to the day of her death in 1894, was an outspoken supporter of all sorts of worthy causes including female suffrage and temperance. Nevertheless, the peculiar garment associated most closely with her name—a species of loose trousers originally gathered round the ankles, although in later designs the gathering rose to the knee or even higher—was well suited to bicycling. A cartoon in a contemporary number of *Punch* fixes the historical scene. 'Please can you tell me the way to Wareham?' asks a female cyclist at fault in a Dorset lane. 'No I can't,' the countryman replies. 'My wife is sticking to a skirt.'

As the nineteenth century closed and the twentieth began, the final advances in the technology of transport were about to emerge. The bicycle fathered two inventions which made the subsequent success of the automobile easier: ball-bearings, and the pneumatic tyre, designed by John Boyd Dunlop, a Belfast veterinary surgeon, out of a piece of garden hose. Again, we see innovations owing little or nothing to science but born in a scientific environment where such articles as steel spheres and rubber tubing are available.

Just as the technology of the second half of the nineteenth century is most vividly exemplified by the steam engine and the steam loco-motive, so is the historical image of the first half of the twentieth century indelibly marked by the development of the petrol-driven motor-car. Both technological events, while essentially dependent on scientific knowledge, are in a large measure side-issues rather than the direct outcome of scientific thinking. The appearance of heavy steam locomotives running on rails naturally led the engineers of the time to turn their minds to the possibility of a machine capable of running on a road. Steam carriages had some success in the 1820s. Sir Goldsworthy Gurney ran several in 1822 and Walter Nancock established steam-driven buses until they were stopped by the law of 1834 decreeing that the speed of every carriage not drawn by a horse should be restricted to $2\frac{1}{2}$ m.p.h., while the vehicle itself must be preceded at a distance of a hundred yards by a man carrying a red flag.

While workable explosion motors were built in France in 1863, the men who finally succeeded independently and almost simultaneously in developing a sound technical design for the machine which was eventually to drive a car were Gottlieb Daimler and Carl Benz in Germany in the 1880s. In 1883 Daimler patented the idea of a four-stroke motor in which a piston first sucked a mixture of air and petrol-vapour into the cylinder; next the piston compressed the gas; then the gas exploded and drove the piston down; and finally the exhausted gases were pushed out of the cylinder. But although other men developed modified designs—Panhard, Levassor and the Peugeot brothers in France, and then Henry Ford in America—the whole business was not particularly scientific. Indeed, automobiles were only accepted as worth serious attention after their potentialities for *sport* had first been demonstrated. At the First International Contest for Carriages without Horses, run between Paris and Rouen in July 1894, 102 cars started and speeds up to 13 m.p.h. were reached. Fifteen petrol-driven cars finished: the first built by Panhard and Levassor, the second by Peugeot Frères. Yet ten years later in 1904 Henry Ford set up a world record on a frozen lake near his home in Detroit, U.S.A., when he drove his own car at 91·4 m.p.h.

The social revolution brought about by Henry Ford was a scientific revolution, but it did not depend so much on the sciences of chemistry, physics or dynamics as on the scientific method as such. The essential feature of science is the intellectual process which it involves. The facts of a situation have first to be assessed clearly and, if possible, quantitatively. Next, the relationship of the facts to each other must be elucidated so that not only can the past situation be understood, but also the principles underlying it can be seen so that the effect of an applied force or reaction can be anticipated. Henry Ford applied this kind of thinking to the processes of manufacture.

The doctrine of the 'division of labour' became more than a theory of economics during the reign of Queen Victoria and was held as an article of faith, enjoying almost metaphysical status: Herbert Spencer, in his book *Progress: Its Law and Its Cause* published in 1857, held it to be an essential ingredient of economic advance and the Prince Consort, quite rightly, gave it royal approval in his presidential address to the British Association in 1859. The 'division of labour' sprang naturally from the success of the factory system when, in a boot factory employing a thousand men, no one man could make a pair of boots while the boots from the factory were cheaper and made quicker than those any one man could make. Ford, however, carried the idea to its scientific conclusion and with his flare for technology mounted the chassis of his cars on a travelling belt. In 1908 he produced 10 cars, each of which cost $850; in 1912 the output of his factory was 170 cars and their price was $600. By 1916 the production of Ford cars—each well designed, standardised, efficient and mass produced—had reached 750 cars and their price was down to $390.

This was the final break between the nineteenth and twentieth centuries. The sciences had begun to move at an accelerating pace in the Victorian age. Knowledge of chemistry, of which metallurgy is a part, made precision engineering possible. Knowledge of physics and mechanics allowed the heat-energy of steam to be effectively applied and controlled. Petroleum was a peculiarly convenient fuel for use in internal combustion or 'explosion' engines, but had petroleum not been available, the same results would have been obtained with gas derived from coal or with hydrogen or alcohol or some other volatile fuel. The impact on the historical scene was due to a combination of all this with, in addition, the ideas of science devoted directly to the process of manufacture itself.

Henry Ford's cars, though technically good, were not strikingly better than those of his contemporaries; indeed, in some respects they were less good. But the Rolls and the Daimlers, the Peugeots and the Delages were fabricated as individual engineering projects and were in consequence, while possessing refinements in certain respects that the Ford cars did not have, slower to manufacture and more expensive. Ford's slogan was, 'Buy a Ford. Your wife can drive it. Any colour you like as long as it's black.' By means of his streamlined, mechanised mass-production, he released a flood of cars which anyone could drive and which more people could afford to own than had ever been conceived before.

To compare a picture of London or Paris, Rome or Berlin in 1913 and in 1923 is instantly to see that a change had occurred in the life of cities of a fundamental significance that no other decade could show. The impact of this social revolution is still being felt today. Residential streets built in the first two or three decades of the twentieth century before the significance of the advent of the motor-car had been appreciated are now choked each night with the stationary automobiles of the people who live in them. The cities themselves— from Tokyo to Chicago—are cut through with broad motorways as impassable as the rivers upon which the ancient cities were founded and which, in their time, served as thoroughfares. The buildings of the later decades of the twentieth century are shaped to take account of motor-cars. It is generally accepted that a large construction, whether it is for dwellings, offices or manufacture, must make provision for the motor-cars of the people who will use it: cities themselves, which evolved from being fortified collections of houses within a wall into civilised centres for culture and commerce, have changed their character because of the historically sudden emergence of motor-cars. Shops round a market square cannot be operated in a motorised society. The people who wish to buy cannot reach them because the approaches and the square itself, designed for the passage of people, cannot cope with people in motor-cars and are choked with traffic. The merchants who wish to sell cannot obtain their goods except by desperate expedients allied to the forbearance of drivers willing to unload merchandise at 4 a.m. In the large towns of the New World, the markets—'supermarkets' as they are being called—are no longer situated in the centre but on the outskirts, where buildings, roads and parking places can be provided specifically to deal with a society in which the motor-car is an integral tool for living.

The first major technological advance in transport, the steam locomotive, brought cities close together. Before their advent little more than a century ago, a mother in Edinburgh, saying goodbye to her son setting out to seek his fortune in London, could expect to be divided from him as completely as would a British mother today whose boy was going to settle in Australia. But a century ago, the cities themselves still retained their integrity, each was a co-ordinated community in which the citizens lived and worked and took their pleasure. But the second technological wave, the crest of which fell on society in the third and fourth decades of the present century, has had a more penetrating impact.

Although history never, in fact, repeats itself, the motorways have reproduced in the twentieth century something of what the railways brought about in the nineteenth. Again, civil engineering has driven great highways across the landscape, taking no account of parish and county boundaries and leaping across the obstacles of geography as only the Roman roads ever did before. But the strings of motor-cars, one behind the other, travelling across France and Germany, Italy, Great Britain, the United States, do not, like the train of carriages following a steam or diesel locomotive, come to a stop in a station when they reach the city of their destination. And this is the main cause of their disruptive effect on modern communities. The trains of motor-cars, motor lorries, petrol tankers, car transporters, caravans and long-distance buses travelling nose to tail from one densely populated place to another enter the towns of their destination and fill up the roads and market squares and open spaces like water filling a sponge. And the vehicles that do this, and by doing so change the whole character of social life, are products of the Second Industrial Revolution. This is the operation in which scientists of all sorts are directly engaged—the chemists to improve glass-fibre bodies bonded with synthetic resins, the physicists to develop new sources of power, materials with greater resistance to heat and fatigue, the biologists to ensure that the amplitude of vibration shall not cause the driver or his passengers physical harm or send them to sleep.

The last main change in transport in the crowded century was, of course, transport in the air. Attempts to fly by means of balloons are of some antiquity. A manuscript in the University of Coimbra described an experiment carried out by a Don Gusmao in which a model balloon, with a flame burning in its gondola, was demonstrated to the King of Portugal in the Salla das Embaixadas in 1709. The balloon rose slowly into the air, drifted against the wall and caught fire.

It was not until more than sixty years later in 1783, that the brothers Montgolfier succeeded in demonstrating that balloons could really fly. On June the 5th of that year—and for quite the wrong reason—they launched a large balloon, 110 feet in diameter and held together by buttons and buttonholes, to a height of 6,000 feet above the provincial town of Annonay. This technological success

65

was admired by the enterprising brothers without a proper knowledge of scientific principles underlying what they were doing. What took the balloon up was the fact that the specific gravity of the heated air in it was less than that of the surrounding atmosphere: the Montgolfier brothers believed that there was some sort of electrical fluid in the mixture of damp straw and chopped sheep's wool which they burnt, and that the smoke from it with which they filled their balloon possessed special powers of levitation. Within two months, however, on August the 27th, 1783, Professor J. A. C. Charles, a real scientist whose work made a serious contribution to knowledge which is valuable to this day, launched a balloon filled with hydrogen to a height of 3,000 feet from the Champ de Mars in Paris.

But although science could provide the knowledge by which the weight of a vehicle and people in it could be lifted up in the air—either by hot air, hydrogen or, later on, by helium—insufficient scientific understanding of aerodynamics, the knowledge of the forces of movement in air, was available to allow a successful airship to be developed which could both float in air and travel through it under its own power. Nor was knowledge of aerodynamic principles sufficiently complete to show that such a development was not feasible. Between 1852, when Henri Giffard in France built a cigar-shaped balloon driven by a light steam engine, and 1939, when the last of the great airships initiated by Count Ferdinand von Zeppelin in Germany was broken up, such vehicles enjoyed a chequered career. One of the final craft, the LZ127 travelled round the world and crossed the Atlantic more than a hundred times. But technology inadequately supported by science is always hazardous and the history of dirigible airships was filled with disasters: some were wrecked by air turbulence and the force of the wind; many of those filled with hydrogen caught fire; others were destroyed by lightning.

Leonardo da Vinci's papers, preserved by Francesco Melzi, showed that da Vinci in the fifteenth century had thought out a rational design for a flying machine, although of course he had not the means to propel it. Three hundred years later at the end of the eighteenth century when ideas for technology were everywhere being mooted, Sir George Cayley, who invented the caterpillar tractor and railway signals, designed several workable man-carrying gliders. A number of other men, mostly amateurs who learned the science of aerodynamics as they went along, followed Cayley. Alphonse Pénaud, who died in 1880, constructed successful models driven by elastic; Louis-Pierre Mouillard, another Frenchman, brought out an excellent handbook on gliding in 1881. Otto Lilienthal achieved considerable feats of gliding before he crashed and killed himself in 1896. A few years later, Octave Chanute, a Frenchman who lived in America, in his book *Progress in Flying Machines* gathered together all that was known of the technology and science of flying. This was available to Wilbur and Orville Wright had they known it during the construction and testing of their power-driven aeroplane which made its first successful flight on December the 17th, 1903.

From that date to the present time, the history of air transport has developed with accelerating velocity. Blériot flew the English Channel in 1909. Two Englishmen, Alcock and Brown, flew the Atlantic in 1919. Jet propulsion took the place of propellers and the speed of sound was exceeded by the American airman, Charles Yeager, in 1954.

Once again as we trace the events of history in the age of science and technology, we come to the same paradox. On land, the capacity of mechanically propelled vehicles has grown increasingly greater. Motor-cars have become capable of higher and higher speeds. Roads have therefore to be specially built to accommodate them. In 1961, the manager of the Department of Traffic in Los Angeles reported that each 'freeway interchange'—that is to say, road junction—occupied 80 acres of land while each mile of road occupied about 30 acres. One third of the total area of the city, he reported, was required for 'transportation facilities'. In spite of the increasing area of roads, however, the vehicles on them grew in numbers even faster. Alternative means of mechanical travel only partially eased the continual tendency towards congestion. Metropolitan railway systems, usually operated electrically, were designed to run under the ground in tunnels, on the surface, or over the surface on raised fly-overs spanning the city blocks.

Sea travel has largely been abandoned for passengers because travel by air is so much quicker but for short journeys a technological development has been the interposition of an 'air-cushion' between the ship and the water to enable the 'hover-craft', as the vessel was termed, to travel faster. This idea may only be of limited use.

In the air, while speeds became faster and the Atlantic, spanned in fourteen hours (with a stop at Newfoundland) in 1950, was flown in seven hours non-stop in 1960, congestion has also become a problem and aircraft, arriving at a busy destination, may be required to wait up to an hour in the air before being able to land. An aeroplane flying round the world—from Copenhagen to San Francisco, let us say, or from Moscow to Tokyo—is not travelling free in the sky. In the 1940s and 1950s, physicists and electronics engineers developed a series of beacons, which are now dotted all over the globe. They usually consist of a 'master' and 'slave' each emitting an impulse which operates the automatic pilots in the aircraft. Thus, wherever an aircraft goes it flies as it were along a 'road' marked and fenced from one beacon to the next.

In a short half-century the technological innovation, the aeroplane, has changed the nature of human society in several respects. Railways linked cities together in the nineteenth century: aeroplanes link nations together—for better or worse—in the twentieth. Queen Victoria's prime ministers could travel from London to Balmoral overnight to obtain her royal approval to their acts. Queen Elizabeth's ministers can—and do—travel to Washington (or Moscow, Pekin or St Helena) overnight to have conversations of equal moment. The airways of the world are truly highways. There are no remote and mysterious places any more. The Plain of Jars, Tashkent, Timbuktu, Thule in Alaska, the South Pole, Goose Bay and Pittsburg—all are equally accessible.

CHAPTER V

LIGHT

The social life of a community possessing electric light is so different from that of a community without it that it comes as a surprise to recall how recent and sudden the development of effective artificial illumination has been. Consider Mr Pickwick, in 1837, going to his bedroom. 'His candle, not a long one when he first received it, had flickered away in the draughts of air through which he had passed, and sank into the socket as he closed the door after him.' He therefore undressed in the dark with such light as was provided by the flickering of the fire. Suddenly, there was 'a most unexpected interruption—to wit, the entrance into the room of some person with a candle'—a middle-aged lady, and 'it was quite clear that she contemplated remaining there for the night; for she had brought a rushlight and shade with her, which, with praiseworthy precaution against fire, she had stationed in a basin on the floor, where it was glimmering away like a gigantic lighthouse in a particularly small piece of water'. Mr Pickwick had mistaken his room.

Here again is an account of Mr John Jorrocks and his huntsman, James Pigg, discussing the next day's sport, which was written in 1843.

About nine Betsey brought the supper-tray, and Jorrocks would treat Pigg to a glass of brandy and water. One glass led to another, and they had a strong talk about hunting. . . . The fire began to hiss and Mr Jorrocks felt confident his [weather] prophecy was about to be fulfilled. 'Look out of the winder, James, and see wot 'un a night it is,' said he to Pigg, giving the log a stir, to ascertain that the hiss didn't proceed from any dampness in the wood.

James staggered up, and after a momentary grope about the room—for they were sitting without candles—exclaimed, 'Hellish dark, and smells of cheese!'

'Smells o' cheese!' repeated Mr Jorrocks, looking round in astonishment. . . . 'Vy, man, you've got your nob i' the cupboard—this be the vinder.'*

* Surtees, R., *Handley Cross*. London, 1854, p. 493.

How completely the technology of artificial light—a technology which this time is firmly based on science—has changed the flavour of life after dark. Even when we move to 1894 and the decade or so that followed and consider the environment in which Sherlock Holmes, one of the first of the scientific detectives, lived, things were very different from what they soon became when light had become a generally distributed municipal utility. Dr Watson handed Holmes a derelict bowler hat of unknown ownership salvaged from the Tottenham Court Road. 'It is perhaps less suggestive than it might have been,' Holmes remarked. Nevertheless he immediately deduced that the man who had lost it was intellectual, had taken to drink, lost his wife's love, led a sedentary life, had grey hair anointed with lime cream. 'Also, by the way,' he concluded, 'it is extremely improbable that he has gas laid on in his house.' He explained his last deduction thus:

> One tallow stain, or even two, might come by chance; but when I see no less than five, I think that there can be little doubt that the individual must be brought into frequent contact with burning tallow—walks upstairs at night probably with his hat in one hand and a guttering candle in the other. Anyhow, he never got tallow stains from a gas jet.*

Here, then, we find candles still used as a means of illumination right up to the end of the nineteenth century, having been developed in much the same form in Roman times—although it is true that the Romans used beeswax. In Paris in the thirteenth century there was a guild of candle-makers, and for centuries candles were made by dipping; first the pith of rushes was used but later on threads of flax or cotton were dipped in the same tallow spoken of by Sherlock Holmes in the 1890s.

Over the centuries candles were slowly improved. The improvement, such as it was, shows the snail's pace of technique when it is unsupported by science. The manufacture of tallow candles could be considered to be advanced as one apprenticed 'chandler' learned from his master. And so the tallow 'dips' were made by immersing the wicks in the melted grease, pulling them out to let the tallow set, and then dipping them in again to increase the diameter of the candle by an eighth of an inch after each immersion. The men who did this in

---

* Conan Doyle, Sir A., *The Short Stories of Sherlock Holmes*, 'The Blue Carbuncle'. London, Murray, 1966, p. 155.

23: Gas-lighting and fog, 1923.

24: Electric lighting, 1960s.

London formed themselves into a Livery Company of Tallow Chandlers. Progress equally slow and unadventurous took place in the making of candles out of beeswax, only this time, owing to the different behaviour of the starting material, the wax was poured over the wicks instead of the wicks being dipped into the wax. Those who followed this art banded themselves together into the Livery Company of Wax Chandlers.

And for all the centuries of time, while skills were learned and apprenticeships served, the rooms of civilised men were gloomy and dark at night. Reading and writing after sunset were a strain on the eyes. An added handicap to study and thought was the distracting necessity of breaking off every few minutes to snuff the wick of the candle.

To leave one's house at night on foot, even in the firmly established civilisation of Europe, was a hazardous adventure. If one could afford to do so, it was prudent and convenient to hire a link-man to light the way with a flaming torch. Certain municipalities issued ordinances instructing townspeople to hang lanterns outside their houses. Others levied a rate for the upkeep of lamps. Just as sailors take note of the tides in arranging their journeys by sea, people would actually attend to the phases of the moon recorded in their diaries and make appointments to go visiting when the moon was full.

The complete and drastic change from inefficient, uncertain and inconvenient lamps, each operating by the combustion of oil or wax, to the quite different order of power and reliability which we accept as one of the commonplace necessities of civilised life demonstrates strikingly well the different levels at which scientific thinking can be brought to bear on practical affairs.

For example, at the end of the eighteenth century Aimé Argand, a French physicist, introduced the glass cylinder which, by improving the efficiency of the combustion of oil taking place at the wick, greatly increased the amount of light from a lamp. The discovery was not made by scientific thought leading to a correct deduction; Argand's young brother happened to be playing with an oil lamp and in the course of his game held a bottle, the bottom of which was broken off, over the flame. Argand recognised the significance of what he saw and put the idea into practice.

A technical advance based directly on science was the use of stearic acid—stearine—in place of tallow. In 1815 Chevreul, a distinguished French scientist whose work laid the foundation of modern understanding of the chemistry of fats, discovered that their molecular structure was made up of a combination of a particular type of alcohol—the sweet, oily liquid, glycerol (also called glycerine) —chemically linked to fatty acids. These fatty acids may be of various molecular sizes and configurations. Some are mobile and liquid at all atmospheric temperatures, others are more viscous and become solid at room temperature. The character of a natural fat, whether it is hard and solid like cold mutton fat or whether it is liquid like olive oil, is determined by the chemical composition of the component fatty acids of which its molecule is composed.

Chevreul worked out a method by which the glycerol and the fatty acids of their molecules could be separated. This was done by churning the fat with a slurry of water and lime or magnesia at high temperature in a vessel like a pressure cooker. When the mixture was allowed to stand, the glycerine 'sweet-water' separated from the combined 'soap' formed by the lime and the fatty acids. The lime-soap was then decomposed with dilute sulphuric acid and the re-formed fatty acids washed and crystallised. Chevreul's scientific studies thus made it feasible to use the harder separated fatty acids which crystallised most readily for the manufacture of candles. These stearine candles possessed two advantages; first, they were firmer and stiffer than candles made from unprocessed tallow and, second, they smoked less, since it is the glycerol in tallow that produces an acrid smoke when combustion is incomplete.

The application of Chevreul's brilliant chemical studies to this practical problem of manufacture represents an early example of much of the research which goes on in modern times. The improvement brought about was significant and would have justified his being employed in the research department of the candle industry, had such been in existence in the early years of the nineteenth century.

Another piece of industrial research also quite in the modern vein was the discovery made in 1825 by another Frenchman, Cambacères, of how to make a wick that did not need constant snuffing. Because candles—and the lamps of antiquity that had existed before them—always had a wick, chemical science was brought to bear, not to do away with this most troublesome of all parts of the candle, but to improve it. This line of attack—improvement rather than outright invention—is followed by the useful middle class of industrial researchers today.

The best wicks in the early nineteenth century were made of cotton yarn carefully plaited. The difficulty was that as the candle burned and the level of the wax fell, the charred wick remained sticking up rather like a match that is allowed to burn to the end, and caused the candle flame to flare and smoke. Cambacères' invention was to flatten the plaited cotton and 'pickle' it in a solution of boracic acid and nitre, or sal ammoniac, or ammonium chlorate. As a result the wick bent over so that its tip came into the hot oxidising part of the flame, where it was completely burned away.

But though the use of science to improve existing techniques is useful and the accumulation of small advances can convert an extravagant, unreliable Puffing Billy into a sleek powerful Flying Scotsman, this is not the kind of thinking from which the big innovations are derived. Stearine candles were still candles. The gas industry was something entirely new. Its forerunner was the technique for handling gases developed mainly by the Rev. Joseph Priestley in the 1770s. As early as 1787 Lord Dundonald had patented a process for making tar by distilling coal. It was noticed that, together with the tar, a considerable amount of gas was produced and this was ignited quite casually by the workmen to give themselves light to work by. Then in 1802 a Frenchman, Leban, had the idea of distilling wood especially to produce gas; he arranged a display of lighting using this gas which, in fact, gave a very poor light. In the same year in England, William Murdock, who was then employed in the engine works of Boulton and Watt, demonstrated how light could be produced by burning coal-gas.

From this time, the original idea having been conceived, successive technologists began to introduce improvement. By 1807 the manufacture of coal-gas was sufficiently established to allow Pall Mall in London to be lit by gaslight. In Germany, Wilhelm Lampadius made gas as a sideline to the operation of a foundry and introduced gas lighting into the city of Freiberg in Saxony in 1811. Then in rapid succession coal-gas as an illuminant was introduced into Baltimore in 1816, Paris in 1817, Berlin in 1826 and Vienna in 1833.

At this stage, however, the technological development of gas lighting had still to overcome several quite intransigent difficulties. To this day, such troubles are still the hard parts of industrial research. The industrial scientist has not only to recognise a scientific discovery when he sees one, he has also to clothe it in hardware and make it useful.

Gaslight in the 1850s possessed two main disadvantages. It was a great improvement over oil lamps for street lighting even though the naked flame flickered and smoked. But for domestic use, the gas flame, though brighter than several candles, could not be so conveniently positioned behind one's chair for reading. It possessed as well a decisive scientific disadvantage: the gas contained a considerable proportion of sulphur compounds which were converted into sulphur dioxide and sulphur trioxide when it burned. This not only made a smell, but the acid fumes damaged the curtains, frills and pelmets with which Victorian sitting-rooms abounded. The chemists soon worked out ways of freeing coal-gas from its sulphur-containing impurities. At first lime was used, and although effective it presented the people making the gas with the problem of how to dispose of quite large quantities of evil-smelling 'gas-lime'. Eventually in 1849 Frank Hills developed a process by which the sulphurous impurities were caused to react with iron oxide.

The discovery which revolutionised the whole situation and which for a time made gaslight the best artificial illumination there was, and put an end once and for all to the predominance of candles, was the gas-mantle. It is interesting to notice that this advance did not merely involve an improvement of an existing technique. It was based on fundamental thinking about the real nature of light. Light, like heat, is a form of energy. When the temperature of a substance is raised, that is to say, when the heat-energy in it reaches a certain intensity, it begins to glow and, in fact, emits some of its energy in the form of light: the hotter a substance becomes, the brighter it glows. It is true that the phenomenon is more complicated than this; for example, a certain material may undergo chemical reaction at a high temperature rather than remain as it was and emit light. Indeed, this is part of what happens in the gas flame of a Bunsen burner; the hottest part of the flame where the gas is undergoing rapid chemical reaction with the oxygen of the air is almost invisible. The bright part of the flame is where particles of carbon, red hot and volatilised, have not yet undergone change.

The flame of a candle is only as bright as it is because it depends on the temperature which the specks of carbon reach just before they vanish as the carbon atoms combine with oxygen: the red-hot carbon at this moment disappears and is converted into the gas, carbon dioxide, which gives no light at all. Candles that burn badly with a smoky flame give less illumination because the light is obscured by particles of uncombusted soot, but no candles give more light per unit volume of flame than any others because the temperature of the flame remains the same. There are two scientific principles that can be used to break out of this impasse: either take steps to produce a higher temperature by using an oxy-acetylene flame, for example, or an electric arc or, alternatively, select some element other than carbon which becomes red hot—or, better still, white hot—at a lower temperature. And this is what C. A. von Welsbach did. Instead of using the gas flame to give *light* from the combustion of the carbon-containing substances in it he used it to give *heat* to make a 'mantle' incandescent.

The emergence of this apparently mundane utilitarian object was, in fact, an astonishingly romantic scientific event. Towards the end of the eighteenth century the genius of such men as Lavoisier and Priestley caused a great jump in chemical discovery. As part of this surge of scientific advance, J. Gadolin separated a new element, a so-called 'rare earth', from a black mineral found in Ytterby in Sweden. He called it yttria. This was in 1794. In 1803 another rare earth, ceria, was discovered from ore mined also in Sweden. Later this was found to be a mixture of lanthana and didymia, and yttria itself was discovered to be a mixture of terbia and erbia. And so the pursuit went on until at least fifteen rare earths, mostly only separated from each other with difficulty, had been discovered. Of these, von Welsbach in 1885 separated didymia into praseodymium and neodymium.

Von Welsbach, in pursuit of purely scientific knowledge, studied particularly one of the peculiar properties of the strange rare elements which were the subject of his research. Sixty years before, in 1826, a chemist called Gurny had observed that if a piece of lime was heated in the very hot flame of burning hydrogen it became white hot and emitted a brilliant light. This so-called 'lime light' was quickly adopted—in a theatre for example—where a very bright beam was needed. It was soon found that instead of using a solid lump of lime a platinum wire coated with lime could be used, or even a piece of blotting paper saturated with a lime solution. The paper burned away but the skeleton of lime remained. Magnesia could also be used in place of lime. There were, therefore, certain precedents when von Welsbach was beginning his researches into the rare earths.

The most difficult part of any study of the rare earths is the problem of separating them from each other. Von Welsbach used a spectroscope to identify his preparations and his technique was to coat a platinum wire with his solutions, heat it over a Bunsen burner and examine the spectrum of light produced. This technique was not very satisfactory; he could not get enough of his solutions to adhere to the wire. So he used a cotton thread dipped in the different solutions of rare-earth salts. Then he noticed that even when the cotton had burned away, the 'cinder' of rare earth retained its integrity. He also observed that it glowed in the gas flame very brightly. Von Welsbach quickly saw the significance of these observations and in 1885 took out a patent for gas-mantles made from lanthanum, yttrium, zirconium—and a year later—from thorium as well.

Von Welsbach's early mantles were not particularly satisfactory. Because it was so difficult to separate the individual elements, the light produced varied in colour a good deal and, though brighter than that of a simple gas flame, was not outstandingly so. He pursued his studies. Hitherto no great trouble had been taken to purify the materials from which his early mantles were made. About 1891 he was working on a method to purify the thoria and observed that the higher the degree of purity the *less* light the thoria emitted. He was struck by the notion—that the brightness of the mantle was not primarily due to the thorium but to a trace of some contaminant. This he discovered to be ceria. The most wonderful light of all, he found—and the discovery has stood to this day—was given by a mixture of 99 per cent thoria and 1 per cent ceria, still called 'Welsbach mixture'.

From being a commercial failure, Welsbach's gas-mantles were now a revolutionary success. The rare earths changed from scientific curiosities of only academic interest into commodities of high economic significance. Sources of supply were sought all over the world and were opened up in Brazil and Travancore in Southern India. At first cotton fibres were dipped in the rare-earth solutions to form the mantles. Soon it was found that better, stronger mantles could be made if 'ramie' fibre was employed in place of cotton; this is derived from the tschuma plant which was imported from China for the purpose. Everything about gas-mantles seems outlandish: to mark the finished mantle with the maker's name, it was found that letters outlined in the rare element, didymium, on the still moist 'stocking' would remain when the mantle was incandescent.

Gas lighting, although it only held its position from the 1890s when the perfection of the gas-mantle made it predominant until electric lamps with osmium and tungsten filaments were developed in about 1911, played a major part in reshaping the social life of the new industrial communities and carrying them into the technological age of the twentieth century. Streets and buildings, domestic houses, workshops and factories were no longer dependent on daylight. In the cotton-mills of Manchester men could now work night shifts and still keep watch over the 840 threads in their looms.

The scientific reason why the amalgam of 99 per cent thoria and 1 per cent ceria gives so brilliant a light when heated is still a matter for research. The theory of 'selective radiation' says that of the energy given off by the mixture a remarkably high proportion is radiated as visible light rather than as heat. An alternative hypothesis postulates that the thoria possesses a poor capacity for radiating heat so that the energy is conserved by the ceria which, therefore, radiates more light. A third theory is that the thoria–ceria mixture acts as a catalyst to raise the temperature of the burning gas and hence increase the intensity of the light. Whatever the true explanation, scientific research on the obscure rare-earth elements led to a technological advance that made a mark on the history of the times.

The development of incandescent electric bulbs is also interesting. Sir Humphry Davy first demonstrated the brilliant light of an electric arc in 1813, but it was not until 1848 that the French physicist, Léon Foucault, lit a square in Paris with arc-lighting for which the current was produced by large batteries. Later, in 1880, when Faraday's scientific discoveries of electromagnetism had been converted into the practical technology of the dynamo, it became a practical proposition to use arc-lighting in streets, markets, railway stations and other public places. These arc-lamps emitted a blinding glare, they burned in open globes producing noxious gases and consumed large amounts of electric power.

On September the 8th, 1878, Thomas Edison paid a visit to the brass foundry of William Wallace and Moses Farmer in Ansonia, Connecticut. There he saw demonstrated an 8-h.p. dynamo which operated eight 500-candle-power arc-lamps. Edison at that time was already a professional inventor with an established workshop at Menlo Park. He was much struck with Wallace and Farmer's electric lighting. At the same time he instantly recognised its drawbacks: it was uneconomic and wasteful of current and—most important—it was quite unsuitable for domestic illumination. He therefore set out to do what is quite common now but was less so seventy-odd years ago—he undertook research aimed at a clearly defined and explicit goal. He set to work to subdivide the intense glare of an arc-lamp into manageable units of electric light which could be 'piped' into people's houses from a central power-house just like gaslight. And in fifteen months of intense effort he succeeded.

Edison was in every way the first of the modern industrial research workers. To start with, he 'sold' his idea to financial backers; they put up the money to enable him to undertake his technological 'R and D'—research and development—which even then was expensive, just as it is now. Again, although his target was a strictly utilitarian one, he possessed a fundamental grasp of the scientific principles by which it could be achieved. For example, arc-lamps have a comparatively low electrical resistance and consume large amounts of current. Edison quickly realised—as his contemporaries had failed to do—that if domestic lamps were operated on this principle the amount of current needed to light a whole house, let alone a street or a town, would be so great that there would not be enough copper in the land to make transmission lines of the necessary thickness to carry the electricity required. Ohm's Law, with which Edison was familiar, relates the amount of current, its voltage and its resistance. Understanding the logic of this piece of scientific knowledge, Edison saw that he would need to use much higher voltages than were then common and greater resistance in his lamps so that the current required could thereby be reduced to a manageable amount.

Having reached his perfectly sound scientific conclusions Edison set himself and his staff to implement them. For a start, finding that the dynamos then in use could not supply a steady output of high-voltage current, he got to work to design and build one which would. His next problem was to discover a wire filament which could be made white hot and incandescent by the current but which would not burn away. First he used a spiral of thin platinum wire, and found that such lamps would burn for 'an hour or two'. To improve this performance he decided to try to obtain a more perfect vacuum inside his bulbs, and he achieved this aim by the remarkably up-to-date process of what is today called 'reading the literature'. While his assistants struggled to improve the equipment he already possessed, Edison was to be found at all hours of the day and night reading reports, scientific journals and the proceedings of technical institutes. As a result he came across a description of the Sprengel vacuum pump. When he tried this machine, which used mercury to trap and expel air, he found that he was able to produce a far more perfect vacuum than he had ever been able to achieve before.

It was while experimenting with ways of making a vacuum in his lamp globes that Edison made a scientific discovery of some importance: that materials which he was testing as substitutes for the platinum wire—and with immense diligence he tried virtually every infusible metal, including iridium, boron, chromium, molybdenum and osmium as well as carbon—often contained oxygen trapped in their pores. When he got rid of this trapped oxygen by heating the filaments while at the same time applying a vacuum, he found that they lasted much longer when made incandescent in the lamps.

By August 1879 Edison had been at work for almost a year on the project. The flavour of his activities was quite different from anything that had been done before his time. Lavoisier in the 1880s had worked hard to outstrip Priestley in discovering the nature of fire and combustion; Faraday had striven to unravel the principles of electromagnetism and hence had developed a practical electric motor and dynamo; but the underlying motives of these men had been to discover the secrets of Nature first and, after that, apply them to practical use. It is true that Watt and Stephenson and, perhaps even more directly, Rudolph Diesel, had aimed directly at making workable useful machines, but their targets were to some degree a matter of faith. Edison was an innovator in that he provided the knowledge and enterprise and the buildings, staff and equipment into which a number of business men had sunk money in the reasonable expectation of reaping a foreseeable profit in a measurable period of time.

After he had been working for nine months and had already spent a great deal of money, Edison felt compelled to organise a demonstration to show his backers—who were beginning to doubt the safety of their investment—the progress he had made. The demonstration was a disaster. At that time he was experimenting with lamps containing filaments made of coiled platinum wire. The dynamo was started, the current was gradually turned on; the lamps began to glow; they got brighter; then one by itself became brilliantly bright; immediately there was an eruption and a puff and the whole workshop was in total darkness.

From then on the tempo of the research was increased to a febrile pitch. The drive to 'deliver the goods' had become desperate. Edison exhibited all his powers of drive, imagination, technical originality and leadership. He pressed on with the work to obtain an improved vacuum. He engaged a German glass-blower called Ludwig Boehm to make globes of new shapes which he designed himself. He investigated a number of ways of inserting the electrical connections and of sealing the bulbs. The improved dynamo was designed partly by Edison's own grasp of principles and flare for identifying the significant targets at which to aim; but it was also dependent on the knowledge of his assistant, Francis Upton, a young electrical engineer who had worked in the laboratory of the distinguished physicist, von Helmholz. This was another modern aspect of Edison's approach—the employment of a highly qualified 'back-room boy'. From all this his most notable success was the development of a workable filament.

When Edison first tested carbon for the filament of a lamp he had been unable to make a fine enough rod; the pieces he examined consequently called for too much current and were impracticable. After testing a series of different metals, partly to see how they behaved when made incandescent and partly to discover whether he could find a means of fabricating them to his purpose, he had fixed on platinum, with the unsatisfactory results which I have already described. At this point, he made his observation that if residual oxygen were got out of the porous structure of the substance making up a filament it resisted heating more effectively. He therefore decided to re-examine carbon. By sheer hard work he made his staff find a way to draw out a very fine carbon filament. To do this, they had to knead lamp-black and tar for hours on end. When they eventually found out how to make a spiral of carbon filament, they had to discover a way of fusing the ends on to the wires carrying the current; next the fragile combination had to be sealed into the globe and evacuated.

At last in December 1879 it was done. The lamp-black and tar had been succeeded first by filaments made of carbonised ordinary cotton thread and later by carbonised paper. Although the experiments had cost in all $42,000, the men who had backed Edison were to get a return for their investment. The bulbs with their carbon filaments gave light and lasted and research and development could now be seen to be a way of making discoveries of economic significance.

Another new aspect in the history of applied science was the fact that technology, as we should now call it, had for the first time attracted popular esteem. Before Edison's time, the work that scientists did was thought of as something mysterious; a few great men attained fame and reputation for their scientific achievements. Now, not the men only, but the operation of research work itself was seen to be something to be admired and applauded. On New Year's Eve, 1879, a crowd of several thousand sightseers came to Menlo Park to inspect the new lights and marvel at them. Besides ushering in a new era of technological living in which people could expect, as a natural thing, to be able to obtain light at the touch of a switch, they also began to expect to be able to command any technological thing they wanted to appear, provided they invested sufficient money and work in having it discovered and built.

Soon carbon filaments were replaced by something better. Magnesium rod and then platinum spirals were made to give light for a smaller expenditure of current; metals which Edison had been unable to fabricate were eventually employed; the rare-earth element, osmium was used and the bulbs containing it were called 'Osram' lamps. Then a way of working tungsten, the metal with the highest melting-point of all, was discovered; tungsten-filament lamps were introduced in 1911.

The technological attainment of electric light introduced a major change into the nature of civilised life. Men and women could for the first time read and write and work as easily in the hours of darkness as in daylight. Gaslight had been a major advance on oil lamps and candles but in the end it could offer no challenge to the convenience, comparative safety and brightness of electricity. Outside the home, electric lighting changed the appearance of cities at night almost beyond recognition. Besides the gaiety and colour it gave to the night scene, it allowed municipal authorities to light the streets which before had been dark and dangerous.

The electric lamp bulbs which today we accept as a matter of course represent a diverse combination of scientific attainments in chemistry and physics. Besides the lamps designed to operate at high voltage from the central supply, others specially designed to be worked from hand batteries have brought about an equal revolution. At the beginning of the twentieth century, Sherlock Holmes and the Scotland Yard detective, Lestrade, lay in wait for the criminals they wanted to capture with dark lanterns in their hands. In these, the lamp or candle was obscured by a metal shutter which could be raised to allow the light to shine out at the crucial moment. At the same time, vehicles at night had to see their way with equally ineffective carriage lamps. Today, automobiles can see to travel at speed in the light of a powerful electric beam. Using the same kind of light, farmers can work in the fields at night if the urgency of the season makes them wish to do so.

Electric lighting is used for a variety of purposes which combine to add a new dimension to life. Doctors use diverse instruments to look into the eye or examine the gastric linings and much else. These instruments all incorporate an electric light. Lights controllable at a distance are used as signalling and alarm devices in industry and commerce. Lights operated electrically control the traffic. Lights in poultry houses make the whole year an eternal artificial spring and encourage hens to lay eggs. Electric lighting reduces the hazards of coal-mining. Underwater lights allow divers to operate in places otherwise impossible for them.

The main impact of electric lighting on the social history of industrialised nations was made in the 1890s when Edison's incandescent lamp began to come into general use. Forty years earlier, however, in 1850, a German physicist, Heinrich Geissler, had made use of an observation recorded as far back as 1675 by Jean Picard; this was that light could be produced by agitated mercury. Geissler took the matter a stage further when he discovered that by discharging electricity through rarefied mercury vapour he obtained bright luminosity. By 1907, an American, Peter Cooper-Hewitt, had devised an effective mercury-vapour lamp. A number of other scientific workers pursued the same principle and by 1934 discharge lamps, as they were called, using lower voltages than the Cooper-Hewitt lamp and filled with gases other than mercury vapour—neon, argon, helium, krypton and xenon—were being developed. The tubes in which the electrical discharge took place were coated with a number of different phosphorescent chemical compounds—so called, phosphors—to obtain improved light of any desired colour. By the 1950s and 1960s such lamps, convenient, economical and cool were coming into increasingly common use.

The next development may well be the generation of light actually within a panel fixed on the ceiling or walls of a room by exciting the phosphors with which the panel will be coated by the direct passage of low-voltage current. This, if it becomes successful, will provide generalised light wherever it is required without the need for lamps at all.

Candles and lamps illuminated the darkness for long historical periods extending over thousands of years, just as the horse maintained unchanged its position as the most rapid means of transport. Then came the sudden efflorescence of thought, the application of scientific principles to practice and, hardly more than a century ago, almost in the memory of old people still living, the gentle, scarce-moving tradition of ages was overthrown. Gaslight in the 1850s ushered in the modern age, held sway for a brief twenty years or so, before being displaced by electric light. The abrupt change had been made, but not as other historical changes of the past, due to conquest, insurrection or natural disaster. The revolution vividly illustrated by the emergence of modern artificial light was due to a sudden modification in the way men directed a certain restricted area of thinking.

CHAPTER VI

MESSAGES

Civilised communities are held together by messages. An organised nation cannot exist unless there are some means by which rapid communications can be maintained between the centre and the outlying parts. Cyrus, the ruler of ancient Persia, could only hold his empire together by a system of posts. Later, when the complex and efficient postal system of Rome fell into decay, the Roman empire of the west came to an end. One of the central features of Oliver Cromwell's efficient organisation of the Commonwealth was the Post Office Act of 1657 which not only allowed him to establish a well-organised administration but also provided his government with the means of discovering and preventing 'many dangerous and wicked designs which have been and are daily contrived against the peace and welfare . . . the intelligence whereof cannot well be communicated but by letter or escript'.

It is interesting to note that, even without the mechanical means which we are about to discuss, the speed with which communications were exchanged was not inordinately slow. A few years after Mr Pitt had established the mail-coach system in 1784, a message could be sent from London to Edinburgh in forty-three hours. Yet even so, this represented a different world from today. Mr Pickwick on his way back from Birmingham and held up by bad weather at Towcester was not able—as we are today—to get in touch with Mr Winkle to let him know the result of his mission. 'I must,' he said, 'send a letter to London by some conveyance, so that it may be delivered the very first thing in the morning, or I must go forward at all hazards.'

The landlord [of the Saracen's Head] smiled his delight. Nothing could be easier than for the gentleman to enclose a letter in a sheet of brown paper, and send it on either by the mail or the night coach from Birmingham. If the gentleman were particularly anxious to have it left as soon as possible, he might write outside, 'To be delivered immediately,' which

84

was sure to be attended to; or 'Pay the bearer half a crown extra for instant delivery,' which was surer still.*

In the modern world, wherever we are we get the news—at once. Public intelligence comes in newspapers. Should a battle be fought half-way round the world, a jet aircraft crash in Tokyo or a civil-rights worker be shot in Mississippi, we can read about them the same afternoon. A merchant can sit in his office and know about the hurricane in Pakistan that will make jute in Dundee dearer. No longer need the traders of Kings Lynn climb to the top of the Guild Hall to watch whether their ships, homeward bound from foreign parts, are at last sailing up the river. A banker can sit at his desk and know at once who is buying sterling and who selling dollars and to what amount.

Beyond the limits of public news there lie private communications. A modern mother in England, saying goodbye to her son departing for Australia, is not losing him for ever. He can let her know when he arrives, write to her each week in the assurance that she will receive his letter in a few days and, if he feels inclined, speak to her by telephone on Christmas Day. A few short generations ago, none of this was possible. Emigration then did in truth mean the end of an old life and the beginning of a new one.

The technological revolution in communications has been as remarkable and fundamental as in any other aspect of life. The prime minister or president who by means of the new methods of communication can keep command of even the complex happenings of a populous and widely extended nation remains none the less a man. And, as such, no matter how widely separated he may be by geography and by the advisers, ministers and generals who surround him, he is still near—in terms of speech—to his adversary. If he lifts the red telephone by his bedside, he can speak on the 'hot line' directly to him.

We have already contrasted the long duration of pre-scientific history with the short time, amounting to little more than a century, during which the scientific idea has been used to guide political action. We have also referred to the suddenness with which the change took place. These questions are particularly cogent when we consider our present topic of telegraphs, telephones and the other speedy

* Dickens, Charles, *Pickwick Papers*. London, Nelson Classics, p. 755.

means of communication which we now have. As with so much of modern technology, the history of these things has two distinct parts: the means by which the practical hardware came into being, and the will which men abruptly developed to want them to be.

What raises man above all the animals, above the bees and ants with their complex, sophisticated and harmonious social relationships, above the seals and dolphins that play together and travel the sea-ways of the world, above the howler monkeys, the colonial societies of the beavers and the charming association of elephants is his power of conceptual thought. Man, as an animal species, can create ideas and communicate them to his fellows by means of the complex, elegant and flexible medium of speech. While it is only in recent times that the full profundity of linguistics—the science of speech—is becoming apparent, the ancients esteemed the value and importance of the art of rhetoric. And rhetoric, the study of the ability to manipulate the spoken word, leads directly to writing which is the art of fixing words on paper so that they become permanent and can be communicated to other men's minds over distances either of space or time.

Even if the ancients held the practical arts, from which experimental science developed, in contempt, one would have imagined that they would at least have devoted themselves to the study of fixing thought on paper—that is to say, printing—and to transmitting thought quickly at a distance. Yet even in these two matters, so intimately concerned with conceptual thinking and philosophy, very little was achieved until the modern revolution of scientific ideas occurred. Pigeons have been kept domestically for immense periods of history: at least since the Fifth Dynasty in Egypt in 3000 B.C. And a pigeon post system was known to have been in operation in Baghdad under the direct authority of the Sultan in A.D. 1150. Yet in spite of its obvious feasibility as a means of rapid communication and regardless of the fact that it does not require scientific or technological expertise, it was never developed, or even revived, after Baghdad was captured by the Mongols in the middle of the thirteenth century. The next time it appears in history as a serious means of rapid communication was in the technological intellectual climate of the nineteenth century. Pigeons were used extensively in France during the disturbed revolutionary period of 1848 for both letters and newspaper despatches. And a little later, in 1849, we hear of their use

25: The post, early nineteenth century.

26: Pigeon post. Airmail before the age of science.

between Berlin and Brussels for the highly practical and up-to-date purpose—of remedying a gap in the electric telegraph system.

Pigeons do not demand any command of technology and neither does the system, used by the Persians in 600 B.C. or thereabouts, of stationing a chain of men with particularly loud voices on promontories across the country so that they can transmit information quickly by shouting one to the next. And the system invented by the Greeks in about 400 B.C. of setting up torches in predetermined positions on a line of towers though ingenious did not require much special apparatus. Yet these methods and others like them faded into disuse during the Middle Ages. Then suddenly there came the new thinking of our own historical period, the intellectual revolution of science, part of which was the desire to discover how things work, but part being the will to do things. And to establish a system of communications was one of the things people wanted to do. Even before complex technological means were developed, the will existed and was of itself successful in getting things done.

In the burst of ideas released by the French Revolution, Claude Chappe brought out his telegraph. It consisted of a 17-ft mast fitted with semaphore arms rather like a modern railway signal. The arms could be set in ninety-two different combinations by means of which the alphabet could be transmitted. On August the 15th, 1794, a line of sixteen Chappe towers between Paris and Lille brought the news of the defeat of Condé by French Republican troops long before a galloping horseman could reach the capital to announce the outcome of the battle by conventional means. The new system could transmit a message over the 130 miles of the system in two minutes—provided, of course, the men operating it had good eyesight, were practised in their work, and there was no fog.

The beginning of the telegraph demonstrated elegantly how intimately the desire and the means are mingled in technological advance. The means to build Chappe's system had existed throughout history, yet it was in fact only developed in the eighteenth century when the *idea* of technology had already taken hold. The electric telegraph also appeared in this same historical period. As early as 1758, an anonymous writer in the *Scots Magazine* made the suggestion that messages might be sent at speed by passing an electric current through a series of wires, one for every letter of the alphabet. And these messages would not be hampered by poor visibility. It was, however, in 1774 that Georges Louis Le Sage actually carried out this idea in Geneva.

Although technology advances when the intellectual climate is favourable, it is never possible to know from whose head the successful idea will come. Modern governments of all advanced nations foster and encourage science in the hope that practical developments of benefit to the nation will emerge. Many new things are originated by setting up commissions and institutes and paying men to work in them. And yet, in the eighteenth, as in the nineteenth and the twentieth centuries, the authorities, no matter how great their civil power might be, could not be sure that the idea they wanted would come to the scientists they hired.

Napoleon in 1809, impressed by the success of Chappe's signalling arms and the code they transmitted, consulted the best scientific adviser he could find: Samuel Thomas von Soemmering. Soemmering was well acquainted with the latest discoveries in the chemistry and physics of his day. He set to work to adapt this scientific knowledge to the elaboration of something entirely new. His telegraph, although it was unfortunately never adopted in practice, was in many ways a monument of ingenuity and elegance. He set up, as Le Sage had done thirty-five years before, one wire for each letter of the alphabet. The novelty of his idea, however, was to tip every wire with a fine gold point with a letter attached and dip each into acidified water. When a current was sent along a particular wire, the water was decomposed by the electricity and a stream of tiny bubbles of hydrogen or oxygen indicated the appropriate letter.

Von Soemmering was a distinguished scientist, the principles he used in his invention were sound, he was the official scientist appointed by the Government—and yet his apparatus was not practicable and was never used. Two more distinguished scientists who worked to develop his ideas and to succeed where he had failed were only partially successful. Professor Karl Friedrich Gauss, director of Göttingen Observatory, jointly with Professor Wilhelm Edward Weber, also of Göttingen, made use of a property of an electric current other than its power to decompose water. They adopted the principle, discovered by Oersted in Copenhagen, that an electric current would deflect a magnetic needle either to the right or to the left depending on the direction of the electric flow. A further and more important novelty introduced by Gauss and Weber was to abandon the use of a separate wire for each letter with a few extra for numerals or punctuation. This inevitably made the apparatus complicated. Instead, they designed a code by which the order in which the magnetic needle was deflected so many times to the left and so many times to the right carried the information. In 1833, they had a workable electric telegraph carried on only two wires from the Observatory to the Institute of Physics in Göttingen.

In 1837, Ernest August, King of Hanover—mark that Bismarck and the German Empire were yet to appear on the scene—brought the enterprise to a standstill. The professors of Göttingen protested publicly—as professors protest to this day—at the King's arbitrary annulment of the constitution of their institute and the King, for his part, exiled the professors from his kingdom. The use of magnetic deflection as a signal was taken up by a number of other workers. In 1835, Paul Schilling, a diplomat at the Russian Embassy in Munich, exhibited at a scientific congress at Bonn a telegraph which he had developed. This had five magnetic needles. Professor Muncke took it to Heidelberg and gave lectures about it. An English student, William Cooke, who had gone to Heidelberg to study—of all things —how to make anatomical wax models, became so intrigued by the Schilling telegraph that he gave up his original plan and returned to England with the specific idea of installing a system of telegraphic communication to allow stations along the then newly developing railway lines to have advance warning of the progress of the trains. It is curious to note how history has to some degree repeated itself. The huge investment in the novel technology of space travel in the twentieth century is sometimes justified by its supporters on the grounds that the incidental 'out-fall'—space suits, liquid diets, solar batteries and the like—provides a variety of novel and useful things which would otherwise never have appeared. Here we see that the lavish investment of money on railways in the nineteenth century—a substantial proportion of which was wasted—also produced its useful 'out-fall'.

When he got back to England, Cooke enlisted the co-operation of an excellent scientist, Charles Wheatstone, professor of physics at London University. Together they organised the building of a four-wire telegraph line operating on the same principle as that used by Schilling. This line extended along the length of the London–Blackwell Railway. Its fame was established with the Victorian public when a murderer named John Tawell who was observed boarding a train at Blackwell was arrested when he alighted at London, the warrant for his arrest having been telegraphed ahead of the train.

For more than half a century, the telegram gave a new dimension to civilised life. The telegraph boy on his bicycle—itself the fastest vehicle on the road—carried in the buff envelope in his pouch messages that might mean life or death. The passage below is from Arnold Bennett's novel *A Great Man*, written in 1904, and well exemplifies an emotional potential that has since ceased to exist.

> Then upon an April morning, the following telegram was received at Dawes Road, Fulham; 'Please bring manuscript me immediately top left take cab Henry'. Mrs Knight was alone in the house with Sarah when the imperious summons of the telegraph-boy and the apparition of the orange envelope threw the domestic atmosphere into a state of cyclonic confusion. Before tearing the envelope she had guessed that Aunt Annie had met with an accident, that Henry was dead, and that her own Aunt Eliza in Glossop had died without making a will. . . .*

The social atmosphere of today, in which technology plays so predominant a part, makes it doubly difficult to feel the atmosphere of an earlier age, so close in historical time yet so remote in its technological differences. In the mid-twentieth century, few people are ever out of earshot of their fellows and there are few places from which it is not possible to communicate. Ships at sea can speak to each other and to the shore, men in battle can seek aid from their commanders, mountaineers on the Matterhorn can discuss their situations for the amusement of spectators at home, policemen on the beat can report to their superiors.

The telegraph was its beginning. In its final and successful form the telegraph made use of a pulse of electricity passing along a wire as the basic signal by which the message was conveyed. But the use of a separate wire for each letter or symbol was too complicated to be practicable. The use of magnetic deflection to the left or right using four wires or even only two was also superseded by something better. The final success has a modern sound to twentieth-century ears.

Samuel Morse, a forty-one-year-old American returning in 1832 in the packet-boat *Sully* from a visit to Europe stumbled as it were by intuition on the idea of using a 'binary' system as the means of

* London, Methuen, 1919, p. 62.

telegraphic communication. Morse did not have any special knowledge of electricity. To be sure, he had 'done' physics when he was a boy at school. But his occupation was that of a historical painter and interior decorator—and not a particularly successful one at that. In fact, in 1832 he was feeling disgruntled with himself through having failed to receive an anticipated commission to decorate one of the rooms in the Capitol at Washington.

During the course of the slow and long-drawn-out voyage across the Atlantic one of the passengers, Professor Charles Jackson of Boston, undertook to entertain his fellow travellers by giving a series of lectures, illustrated by demonstrations, about the recent publication by Michael Faraday of his striking new discoveries of electromagnetism and their application in practice to such ends as, for example, the electric telegraph. It is salutary to recall how interested members of the ordinary educated public—including such men as Samuel Morse—were in scientific matters a century ago. And their interest was not casual, frivolous and undiscerning, as today one might say, 'How interesting!' without in fact taking the least intellectual trouble to think about the matter or being at all interested in it. Morse was greatly struck by what Professor Jackson had to say and turned the ideas over in his mind. And he did more. Three years later he actually constructed an apparatus out of one of his old picture frames. This arrangement used an electromagnet to cause a pencil to move over a paper tape and thus draw an undulating line.

The novelty of Morse's idea was not so much in the electrical circuitry but in his conception of how a message could most simply be sent. Morse in his code hit upon the fact that all the letters of the alphabet and, indeed, numerals or any other 'bit' of information could be identified in a 'binary' language. The Morse code uses only two signals, a dot or a dash, but by simple combinations and sequences of these two any message can be conveyed. It is a remarkable twist of history to find this same supremely simple system being used in modern times to carry information in general-purpose electronic digital computers.

Morse suffered all the troubles and difficulties that have afflicted inventors through the ages. Having got his stylus to work and draw a line, the waves in which showed the position of the dots and dashes, he found that his original apparatus could not send a signal through a wire longer than fifteen yards. Luckily he was able to enlist the co-operation of Professor Leonard Gale of New York City University who, by a coincidence, lived in the same building as he did. Next, he found a gifted technician, a man called Alfred Vail, who, besides his own talents, possessed a wealthy father willing to invest money in the project. By 1837 the Morse telegraph was launched and found to be able to send messages successfully over a distance of 10 miles. Every ingredient of the romantic success story beloved of the Victorians was there. Even after the initial success of the apparatus, there was a period of six years when nobody would buy the Morse equipment and Morse himself was compelled to return to painting to make a living. Finally, success came. In 1843 he was awarded a contract by Congress of $30,000 to build a telegraph line from Washington to Baltimore and his fortune was made.

From then on he enjoyed extravagant success equal to that of an idol of the entertainment world, and for rather the same reason. It was not solely for the superiority of his equipment over that of his rivals that he became Director of Telegraphs of the United States and a professor, or that he received an honorarium of 400,000 francs from ten European countries, or that in his eightieth year two statues were erected in his honour. A major part of Morse's resounding fame was due to his having conceived the idea of the 'Morse Code', that is, the elegant notion that all thought can be communicated in terms of two signals: a dot and a dash.

Morse's original code was not exactly the same as that used today. When the first European telegraph line employing the Morse system was built in 1848 between Hamburg and Cuxhaven—to take the place of a chain of Chappe signalling towers—the inspector of the line, one Gerke, improved the Morse code and, by doing so, did more than anything achieved by the dozen or more electrical engineers who spent their time trying to improve the circuit or the recording gear. In fact, it was Gerke's perfection of the Morse code on top of the excellence of the original idea that was really responsible for the rapid spread of telegraphy across land and later across the sea as well.

Gerke did away with Morse's wavering line with its peaks and replaced it by true dots and dashes. He also established the exact code to be used on a logical basis related to the frequency with which the different letters are used.

From the mid-nineteenth century onwards, the progress of telegraphy consisted of a series of technical developments and improvements, for sending messages, for recording messages, for sending and recording a number of messages simultaneously over a single wire. One curious feature of this progression of advance is worth mentioning. In the early years, when methods for recording telegraphic messages were still being worked out, Alfred Vail made the discovery that a practised operator could learn to read messages by sound and that the Morse code, in spite of its basic simplicity of merely long and short pulses arbitrarily arranged, could be mastered and understood like a language.

The telegraph changed the flavour of the life of the second half of the nineteenth century. But, though remarkable in the increased speed it gave to communications, it was, in its way, only an extension of the public post. One wrote a message on a form, took it to the telegraph office and then waited for a reply. The next step in technological communications was different in kind: the telephone represented an extension of a human sense such as had never been conceived before. Whereas the telegraph is a public service, the telephone enables two people at a distance to communicate privately with each other. Before it existed, people would write long, carefully composed and seriously considered literary letters; after it was invented these were no longer written. The literary art of letter-writing was no longer needed and consequently came to an end.

It is curious that the telephone came into existence in a way that was remarkably similar to the beginnings of the telegraph. Alexander Graham Bell, like Samuel Morse, was no expert in science, nor was he an electrical engineer. Both his grandfather and his father, Melville Alexander Bell, were authorities on elocution and phonetics. His father was deeply concerned with the welfare of the deaf and when he moved from Edinburgh to accept a professorial chair in London in 1867, Alexander, then twenty years old, went with him as his assistant. He worked mainly on an instrument designed to make sounds visible to show deaf-mutes how to speak.

In 1870, two of his brothers died of consumption and his father was warned that he too would succumb unless he were taken to a healthier climate. The whole family therefore moved to Canada to a small estate near Brentford in Ontario. He quickly obtained a post as teacher in a school in Boston and the following year became Professor of Vocal Physiology in Boston University.

The drive, vigour and talent shown by Alexander Bell, particularly during this period of his career, make him a model and example of his age. By his total absorption in 'visible speech' and his lecturing he had already gained sufficient reputation to earn his place at the university. He devoted himself to helping deaf children and for three years lived with the family of a Mr Thomas Sanders in order to be able to teach their deaf son. At the house of another Boston family, he met the daughter, Mabel Hubbard, who had been deaf since childhood and whom he subsequently married. Besides his energetic teaching and lecturing, besides an altruism and devotion to the deaf, he continued working and experimenting on his machine to demonstrate visibly the modulations produced in speaking. His 'phonautograph' was a device in which a bristle attached to a stretched membrane would make a pattern on a smoked glass when the membrane was exposed to different sounds. Later, when a medical acquaintance procured him a human ear from a cadaver he incorporated this in the machine in place of the membrane. Another device was a 'manometric capsule' in which a flame was made to flicker in accordance with the vibrations of a speaking voice. But on top of all this, with the boldness characteristic of the intellectual climate of his times, he was also working on a model of what he hoped would be an improved multiple telegraph. Indeed, his first patents were for a multiple telegraph consisting of a set of reeds connected by a wire. The reeds vibrated at different frequencies. The idea was that a message sent by a reed vibrating at one frequency would only be picked up at the receiving end by another reed vibrating at the same frequency.

Strangely enough it was from the pursuit of the multiple telegraph that his idea for a telephone arose. On any logical basis of planned technological research it would be argued that a professor of vocal physiology had no business to be spending his time on an instrument which was being actively developed and improved by competent, well-trained and experienced electrical engineers. His success—not in improving the electric telegraph, to be sure, but in conceiving something different although related—is a striking example which has been repeated on a number of occasions in the last hundred years of the way original ideas may come from the combination of two apparently unconnected areas of thought. Bell was working on his multiple telegraph with a young technician, Thomas Watson, whom he had first met in the workshop of a Mr Charles Williams where he was accustomed to have his models built for him. The year was 1874. Watson touched one of the reeds of the instrument to transmit to Bell who was upstairs. Bell noticed that the sound emitted from the receiver of the instrument was not only the main tone of the sending reed but also contained the overtones as well. His special training in elocution and his exceedingly accurate ear enabled him to catch the exact combination of tones and the flash of genius he possessed made him recognise the significance of what he was hearing. He realised that an instrument that could produce both the tones and the over-tones of a reed might also be made to transmit the vibrations of the human voice.

Bell and his assistant Watson devoted all their energies to redesign the instrument to operate as what would now be called a 'telephone' rather than as what had been intended to be a telegraph capable of discriminating between messages sent at different harmonic fre-quencies. In 1875, they produced a first rough model. In the following year, 1876, the history of telephone conversation began.

For almost a year, since the time of his first conception of a telephone, Bell had been devoting almost his whole time to it. He was in consequence hard pressed for money. He obtained support from friends; he attempted to get advance payment from the School of Oratory in Boston for lectures that he had not yet delivered. Yet he could not find out how to convert the separate notes that he sent from his transmitter to his receiver into intelligible speech. He carried out a variety of trial-and-error experiments jointly with his assistant, Watson. All this again exemplifies the paradox of technology which while to a major degree based on science is also dependent on effort, skill, patience and intuition. Just as the history of science has its fable of Newton and his apple, the history of technology contains the anecdote of Alexander Graham Bell spilling the acid.

On March the 10th, 1876, Bell was proposing—for no logical reason, as it seemed—to try the effect of a new transmitter in which a stronger undulating current than had been used before was being derived from a galvanic battery. He was in one room, his assistant Watson in another. Just as the new circuit was to be tested—so the story goes—Bell spilt some of the acid from the battery on his clothes and exclaimed: 'Mr Watson, come here: I want you.' To his surprise, Watson in the other room heard Bell's voice distinctly from the transmitter of the machine.

95

The Bell telephone was patented only a few hours before a rival design was entered at the Patent Office in Washington; the application was granted on March the 3rd on the twenty-ninth birthday of the inventor. By 1877, Bell and Watson completed a successful conversation over a distance of 2 miles between Boston and Cambridge. In the same year, Sir William Thomson, later to become Lord Kelvin, was impressed by a demonstration of the telephone at the International Centennial Exhibition held at Philadelphia. In January 1878 when Bell was in England on his honeymoon, he received a command from Queen Victoria, who had heard about his lectures and demonstrations, to show her the operation of his telephone at Osborne House on the Isle of Wight. Not only did he describe the principles of the telephone to the Queen with the aid of models, but he also enabled Victoria to speak to Princess Beatrice and Sir Thomas Biddulph who were at Osborne Cottage. That evening the Queen wrote in her diary of having seen and heard the telephone, 'A Professor Bell explained the whole process, which is the most extraordinary.' How rapid had been the development of science and the drive of able men to apply scientific ideas to practical affairs in the seventeen years since 1861 when the Prince Consort had died of 'congestion of the lungs' at the age of forty-four.

At first, the significance of the telephone was not realised. Bell himself in his lectures used to sing songs into the transmitter. In 1878, people in London paid a penny to talk to a man on the top of one of the City churches and The Times described the instrument as 'An American humbug'. In 1879, the first telephone exchange was opened in London with eight subscribers.

Bell is a striking example of the way in which men imbued with the spirit of discovery, so peculiarly characteristic of the hundred years of applied science with which this book is concerned, possess the urge to discover without any specially strong commitment to the significance of their discovery. He had devoted immense effort and suffered considerable hardship and privation while struggling to perfect a telephone. When it at last became established as a resounding success and he had been awarded the Volta prize of 50,000 francs by the French Government, quite apart from the material rewards from the Bell Telephone Company and the Western Union, he had little further interest in it. By 1880, he had ceased to take any active part in the development of telephony.

He used the 50,000 francs of the Volta prize to found the 'Volta Bureau for the Diffusion of Knowledge for helping the Deaf'. He became interested in the purposeful breeding of selected individuals to improve the human race and was made Honorary President of the Second International Eugenics Congress. He founded the periodical *Science*, which is today the weekly journal of the American Association for the Advancement of Science. He was one of the founders of the National Geographical Society. He started the Aerial Experiment Association, designed and built a kite 42 feet long which was capable of carrying a passenger and produced—this was in 1908—a successful glider. He designed a motor-boat with a speed of over 70 m.p.h. An invention of his for detecting metal in the human body was used to locate the bullet with which President Garfield was shot in 1881.

Mechanical power was the mainspring of the Industrial Revolution. And out of the Industrial Revolution sprang the new era of history of which the last hundred years constitutes the first century. Aldous Huxley, with the acute eye of the creative artist, dated the beginnings of the Brave New World as so many years 'A.F.'—after Ford. Mass-production was only one step beyond the steam engine, which gave one workman the power of thousands. The telephone supplied men with a further dimension. With it they could convey thoughts and commands, not only to people who were in the same place as themselves, but to others situated at a distance. In 1877, the New York *Tribune* scored a resounding success over its rivals by gathering election results directly by telephone while the other papers were still dependent on telegrams. The Berlin Postmaster-General set up a public telephone service in the same year and crowds of purchasers swamped the firm of Siemens and Halske, who were producing telephones at a fraction the cost of those made in America because Bell had omitted to take out a patent in Germany. By 1888, the Berlin exchange was connected to 8,000 subscribers.

Apart from its value to the police and to public departments of government, the telephone soon began to exert an influence on the whole structure of the life of communities in cities. It was no longer necessary for traders to cluster their offices close together; with the telephone they could work at a distance yet keep in touch. The speed of business and commercial life could be accelerated. When Alexander Graham Bell died in 1922, the telephone was almost the commonplace it is today. Telephone wires knitted the human hive together into a closely woven community.

Bell had lost interest in his telephone because, like an artist who when he has finished one picture is only happy when he has started on the next, his energies were fully extended in other directions. What concerned him was the urge to drive on towards new technical innovations rather than involvement with the significance of the innovation itself. It is curious to us, however, with our present hindsight, to trace from the history of the telephone the blindness of many of those in authority to the social importance of the instrument even at the time when its use was spreading rapidly throughout the civilised world. In the year 1880, a single enterprise, the United Telephone Company, came into existence to supply a service in Great Britain. The company itself supplied the telephone service in and around London and licensed other concerns to do the same in provincial cities. The Post Office then brought an action to prove that the telephone was, in the eyes of the law, merely a form of telegraph and consequently any private company installing telephones was infringing the monopoly over telegraphs which the Post Office possessed. Having won his case, the Postmaster-General only permitted the United Telephone Company to install telephones under licence. Until 1884 these licences were only granted with sparing reluctance. It seemed to the Post Office to be more in the public interest to protect the dwindling revenues of the telegraph service rather than encourage people to use the new technological development and speak to each other on the telephone. Then, when the utility of the telephone had at last become manifest to that part of the State represented by the Postmaster-General and he had relaxed the licensing policy, Parliament declined to limit the freedom of individual land-owners to refuse to grant way-leave to the telephone wires. And even in 1892 when the Postmaster-General was granted powers to carry the wires from place to place, these powers could only be used with the concurrence of the local authorities. And some local authorities disliked the Telephone Company and refused their permission. By 1895, these competing social forces were producing complaints from both sides. Another Act was then passed authorising local authorities to run their own telephone services, if they wanted to, in competition with the Company. Only in 1911 did the British community come to terms with the new science-based means of communication. In that year, the State bought up all the telephones from the Telephone Company for £12,500,000 and undertook to run the service for the nation.

The history of the technological revolution in communications was made up of the individual contributions of creative men. Samuel Morse was one of many at work on the telegraph. Alexander Graham Bell's patent only preceded that of Elisha Gray by a few hours. Guglielmo Marconi, who first succeeded in transmitting radio signals in December 1894, had based his design on the work of the German physicist, Heinrich Hertz, the Frenchman, Edward Branly, who developed the 'coherer' from which the radio detector emerged, and on the ideas of a Russian scientist, Popoff, who discovered the efficiency of an aerial as a transmitter.

By 1911, the flood of innovation was in full spate. By passing electrical signals along conducting wires, first the telegraph and then the telephone had become possible. While these applications of electrical conductance were being worked out, a number of other scientists had been studying 'free' electrical waves. In 1865, and in a later communication in 1873, J. Clerk Maxwell had shown that there were electrical emanations which passed through space in the form of a disturbance travelling at the speed of light. Fifteen years later in 1888, the German physicist, Heinrich Hertz, showed that these electromagnetic waves behave in much the same way as light and heat and worked out the mathematical basis by which their effects could be described. These were the premonitory advances in scientific understanding which led to the technological achievement of Guglielmo Marconi in 1896 when he transmitted a 'wireless' signal over a distance of $1\frac{3}{4}$ miles. The following year a message was sent 18 miles from the shore to a ship at sea.

After the basic notion that electromagnetic waves, freely diffusing through space, could be used to transmit signals, progress advanced at a gallop. The technique of transmission and reception continuously improved. The signals themselves, first used as telegraphic morse code, were quickly harnessed to the transmission of speech, and in 1927 they were adapted to the dissemination of television pictures.

The first transatlantic cable capable of transmitting telegraph messages in morse was opened in 1866. Sixty-one years later in 1927, the first transatlantic circuit capable of transmitting the more sophisticated signals of spoken telephone messages was inaugurated.

This was not a cable but a radio-telephone. It was not very reliable because when it was installed it was already well known that radio waves could only be propagated round the curved circumference of the earth by bouncing them off one or other of the several 'shells' of ionised particles by which the globe is surrounded. And these shells are sometimes incomplete and allow messages to leak out into space through the holes in them. Only in 1956 was a reliable telephone cable laid across the Atlantic.

But now in the 1960s the advanced technology of the times seems to be leading to another step forward. Radio waves are in many respects more flexible than waves carried by wires. By making use of rocketry, it has become possible for the communications authorities to put a satellite into orbit to travel round the earth once a day; that is to say, to remain stationary overhead and be always on hand to receive radio signals and reflect them back round the curvature of the earth. Four such satellites circling at an altitude a little above 22,000 miles would allow messages to be transmitted to anywhere on earth.

CHAPTER VII

TECHNOLOGY AND INDUSTRY

'A new civilisation, not only for England but ultimately for all mankind,' wrote G. M. Trevelyan in his *British History of the Nineteenth Century*, 'was implicit in the substitution of scientific machinery for handwork.' With this we can certainly agree as we also can with Trevelyan's puzzlement at why it was that mankind—led, perhaps, by the British but not by very far—suddenly made the substitution. The Greek scientists of Alexandria, the contemporaries of Archimedes and of Euclid, as Trevelyan went on to point out, were good scientists and powerful thinkers but too 'high-souled', it seemed, to consider with anything more than contempt the industrial arts conducted by their slaves. 'In any case,' as Trevelyan puts it, giving up the struggle to understand how it came to happen, 'it was left to the peaceful, cultivated but commercially minded England . . . to harness philosophical thought and experiment to the commonest needs of daily life. The great English inventors negotiated the alliance of science and business.'

It is interesting to recall that the first major 'science-based' industry was cotton. The element of science that gave cotton its impetus and increased the output of the British cotton industry a hundred-fold between 1760 and 1831 was the steam engine. Mills had been worked before by water power, but with the technological advantage of steam power at their disposal they became enormous. The owners turned into modern-style capitalists, the workers were collected in the mills in hundreds, women and their children worked under prison-like conditions for fifteen hours at a stretch all day and lived in street after street of ugly, narrow, insanitary, cheap houses thrown up on behalf of their employers by jerry-builders, 'divorced from nature but unreclaimed by art'.

Cotton manufacture, carried along by the scientifically generated power of steam and aided in England by the happy combination of abundant cheap coal—made cheap in its turn by steam power—and of iron and steel, which themselves depended on the ample supply of coking coal, and of ports convenient to the supplies of cotton together with the humid rainy climate of Lancashire, increased and grew prosperous. The injection of science at the one point only of the steam engine was not sufficient to maintain the prosperity of the cotton manufacturers indefinitely. The cotton industry *used* science but the cotton masters did not *understand* the nature of science. Their machines for spinning and weaving were ingenious and effective but, of themselves, not particularly scientific. The new chemical dyes which came into use were taken up by the cotton manufacturers but did not owe their development to their efforts. Indeed, after a strikingly promising start, the scientific momentum of the British chemical industry was soon lost, as we shall discuss later. The British chemical manufacturers like the owners of the cotton industry failed for much of the nineteenth century to appreciate the fact that the essential nature of science was the constant need to think and re-verify accepted notions.

Cotton, after having increased and prospered mightily in the first few decades of the nineteenth century and held its own by sheer weight of size and expertise to the end of the century, then dwindled and fell on hard times. By the 1920s and 1930s, the unsystematic and unscientific nature of the industry—as distinct from some of its machines—was becoming apparent. The factories, which had been new in, say, 1870 had become old-fashioned but were still in use. One firm did the spinning, another firm applied 'size' to the thread to facilitate the movement of the shuttle back and forth and reduce chafing and friction during weaving, a third firm then operated a process to 'desize' the cloth so that yet another undertaking could dye and 'finish' the pieces. The drama of the brave new technological revolution of the 1830s had evaporated.

Then, in the twentieth century—in our own times—history repeated itself with a new twist. Scientific thinking was applied in a new, more fundamental, way to the problem in hand. Whereas before, to keep the cotton industry prosperous efforts had been made to improve the machinery by which cotton it was spun and woven, or to produce new and more efficient ways of dyeing, sizing, desizing or finishing, in the second and third decades of the twentieth century consideration was given to what it was that constituted a useful textile fibre. And out of this basic reflection, scientific ways were developed to produce new kinds of fibres with properties which made

27: The electric telegraph of 1902, one of the first signs of the new era.   28: A 'crystal set', the radio receiver of the 1930s.

29: The N.A.S.A. sphere, a communications satellite launched in America in 1960. Already obsolete.

them superior to cotton. The great cotton mills of the nineteenth century, which brought wealth and employment, squalor and a new class of skilled technicians—the aristocracy of labour—withered away in less than a hundred years. In their place there are growing up at this moment great chemical works, expensive and elaborate, situated within range of petroleum supplies which are their source of raw material, from which come the nylon and orlon, the terylene and dacron which are the improved scientific successors of natural fibres. These factories employ numbers of people, to be sure, but not so many in proportion to their output as the cotton mills of the previous century. And the kind of people they employ are different. Many of them are better educated, some of them are qualified chemists with university degrees, more of them possess qualification in science, less taxing than those attained by academic graduates but demanding serious scientific study nevertheless—so-called National Certificates and Higher National Certificates and the membership of professional and scientific associations. The comparison of the cotton worker of the 1800s and the technician in a chemical plant making synthetic fibres epitomises the march of history over the critical century from, say, 1850 to 1950 when science became adopted as an essential and major factor in the thinking of industrial nations.

Organic chemistry, that is the chemistry of carbon compounds of which the whole of biological creation is constructed, hardly existed as a science prior to 1850. Charcoal burning cannot be described as a chemical operation although its purpose is to prepare a comparatively pure form of granular carbon. Starch making—although it would be better described as the separation of the chemical compound, starch, from other components of the rice or maize from which it is prepared—is not particularly chemical or scientific either. And the production of alcohol can hardly be claimed as arising from chemical thinking. Then, quite suddenly, in the 1840s and 1850s there was a spectacular outpouring of intellectual genius originating mainly in Germany which led to some of the great social changes we have already discussed. The distillation of coal-gas from coal, seemingly so industrial an operation, led to the study of coal-tar and the separation from it of large numbers of organic chemicals of diverse sorts. The elucidation of the molecular configuration of the members of this group of substances—of benzene, naphthalene and anthracene, of aniline and toluene and a hundred others—led to the discovery of

H   103

the structure of organic chemical substances in all their elegant complexity. And from these apparently theoretical and academic studies emerging from the primitive laboratories of such brilliant experimenters as Gmelin, Liebig, Wohler and Bunsen—natural philosophers who drew to themselves little groups of disciples from all over the world, who learned by working with them and carried away not only knowledge and instruction but love for their masters and for the science they served, and spread it to universities in all the civilised nations of the Western World—from these esoteric studies, great social consequences accrued. Synthetic dyes were developed which ruined the Indian indigo growers and the traders who brought the indigo to the markets of Europe. Synthetic drugs were made and anaesthetics like chloroform and ether which, as we have already discussed, changed men's ideas about pain, life and death; the new explosives, TNT, picric acid, dynamite, fulminate of mercury we have also discussed.

Although chemistry as a whole, as a modern systematic science, only dates from the middle of the nineteenth century when John Dalton established the principle of atomic weight and Mendeléev developed the idea of all the elements on earth being classifiable in a Periodic Table, the origin of inorganic chemistry can be argued as dating farther back in history than that of organic chemistry. The classical chemists knew a great deal about metals and minerals and salts of different kinds. Organic chemistry, on the other hand, was to a large degree hampered by mystical ideas about the allegedly special magical nature of life-produced materials. Thus, when organic chemistry did begin, it began with a specially dramatic rush. Nevertheless, at first, the standards of judgement used by inorganic chemists were adopted by the organic chemists as well. For instance, they took pains to establish the molecular weight of the compounds they were studying and they liked to be able to determine their boiling points and freezing points. Quite soon, however, it became apparent that the chemistry of living substances themselves and the components out of which they were built needed a different kind of understanding.

Cellulose is the main component of cotton. Cotton is made up of long fibres—this is why it can be twisted into thread—and these fibres in their turn are composed of long molecules. While the notion that a molecule of salt (sodium chloride) has a particular molecular weight is accurately reflected by the observed facts of chemistry, the conception of a fixed molecular size for a molecule of cellulose—which has a shape roughly comparable to a piece of string—is less rational and only roughly fits the facts of Nature. Chemical manipulations could be carried out with cellulose, but tidy formulae to describe what happened were not very satisfactory. In 1889, a French chemist, Chardonnet, found that if he treated cellulose fibres with nitric acid under appropriate conditions, a syrupy liquid was formed. This could be forced through fine holes to produce fibres and these could be spun to yield 'artificial silk'.

The first artificial silk possessed a chemical composition closely similar to guncotton and was highly inflammable, just as the first celluloid collars had a pronounced tendency to burst into flames. By 1892, however, Cross and Bevan had succeeded in modifying the process to produce 'rayon', and science could be said to have been applied successfully for the first time to textiles. This was no longer merely the use of engines to operate magnified hand looms.

Artificial silk was prepared by carrying out chemical manipulations on a natural polymer, a very large molecular compound made up of repeating units each of smaller molecular size. This polymer is cellulose. The ability to handle natural polymers led inevitably to the discovery of how to synthesise entirely artificial polymers specially designed to possess particular properties. In the 1930s, the great industrial firm of Du Pont de Nemours in America set out on a deliberate search for a synthetic fibre which should not depend on a natural polymer for its origin. They engaged Dr Wallace Carothers, then a lecturer at Harvard University, to lead a large research team, installed him in a laboratory with every scientific facility he could possibly need—and left him to think. In this particular instance, the operation was successful. After years of work and the expenditure of millions of dollars, and after Carothers himself was dead, Du Pont in 1940 put nylon on the market. And by doing so, they showed that scientific thinking could profitably be applied directly to industrial problems.

The chemistry of polymers from which are derived the whole wide range of 'plastics', including Bakelite, polyethylene, polyvinyl chloride (PVC) and many others has had a profound effect on social history. Plumbers, whose very title implies that they work with lead, must change their trade to handle plastic water pipes; motor-car bodies, brush bristles, watch glasses, electric-light switches—these and a whole variety of articles have come to be made out of the products of chemical industry we call plastics.

But the historical significance of the impact of science on manufacture has had a more important aspect than that due to the development of new things, striking and important though such developments have been. The main change brought about by science and the technology derived from it has been due to the injection of scientific thinking into the actual organisation of industry itself. The basic nature of the scientific process is a continuing doubt. Robert Boyle chose well when he selected *The Skeptical Chemist* as the title of his book. Scientific knowledge advances when people doubt what they are told and design experiments or tests to see whether it is true. And if they find that what they previously thought to be a fact is not exactly so, or that an accepted explanation for a group of facts does not fit the truth of the matter, then it is up to the scientist to make more accurate observations of the fact or to conceive out of his inner consciousness a better explanation to co-ordinate what he has observed of Nature.

Not long ago, the doctrine upon which industry was based was one entirely remote from the challenging philosophy of science. The principle of there being a master with his apprentices, or a guild or society of tradesmen into which newcomers could only enter after serving a novitiate is the very opposite of science. An apprentice serves his master for a number of years during which time he learns the ancient art or mystery of weaving or baking or printing or whatever the operation may be. In due time, he in his turn teaches a younger man what he learned. This process allows a bootmaker, let us say, to make an excellent pair of boots but it does nothing to progress the art of bootmaking which, when the old bootmaker retires or dies, is in exactly the same state as it was when he learned the trade as a boy. Even the introduction of a new kind of tan or an improved quality of thread makes little or no change in the bootmaking process.

In the nineteenth century, as the scientific atmosphere gradually began to pervade more and more aspects of life, things began to change. The idea that to make a particular article—a pair of boots, a copper kettle or a piece of cloth—was a craft that had to be laboriously acquired in a period of training extending over years was gradually replaced by what the economists of the day called 'the division of labour'. Instead of one seamstress making a shirt, a number of women, each now equipped with a sewing machine, made a part of a shirt—and another woman assembled the various portions into the final finished garment. This process of operation quickly extended to almost every kind of manufacture. Before long the doctrine of the division of labour had transcended the works of the economists and was adopted as a Victorian article of faith, enjoying almost metaphysical status, by every reputable business man and manufacturer. Cardinal Newman, the great teacher and theologian, acknowledged its force. Herbert Spencer, in a book called, *Progress: Its Law and Its Cause*, published in 1857, claimed it to be not only a useful technical device but an essential feature of progress itself. Even the Prince Consort, in his Presidential Address to the British Association for the Advancement of Science at Aberdeen in 1859, gave it Royal approval.

The significance of the division of labour which justified the respect paid to it by nineteenth-century manufacturers was that it represented the beginnings of the application of scientific thinking to the organisation of industry and not merely to the processes used. This meant that manufacture was no longer based on the laboriously learned methods of the past but on experimentally established procedures which were liable to further immediate change should they be found on trial to be capable of improvement.

The final development of this phase of science-stimulated factory management was introduced by Henry Ford in 1914. At first, Ford merely arranged for a small belt to carry the magnetos along a table at which sat a number of operators, each of whom had one simple thing to do. A man—or woman—might even be engaged all day long in slipping a washer over the projecting end of a screw; the next man sitting beside him would then put a nut on to the screw, his entire time being spent in putting nut after nut on to screw after screw; then another man would screw the nut on. In due time, however, Ford began to think out the nature of the motor-car-making process as a whole as if it were a scientific problem. And soon he conceived the idea that the moving assembly line could be applied also to the assembly of the car chassis and that then a further assembly line could just as effectively be set up to assemble the body and another to assemble the now completed body with the completed chassis.

Whereas before this original idea was introduced it had taken 12 hours and 35 minutes of work to put a Ford car chassis together, seven months after the moving assembly belt process had been introduced a completed chassis came off the belt every 84 minutes.

Ford's idea of applying what amounted to scientific thinking to industrial production without adhering to any preconceived notions about how a motor-car or, for that matter, a biscuit or a glass bottle *should* be made by a craftsman trained as an apprenticed engineer or biscuit-baker or bottle-maker enormously increased the efficiency of manufacture and consequently reduced prices and made what had previously been luxury articles attainable only by the few available to many more people.

Ford and his mass-produced motor-car represent the crest of the wave of the First Industrial Revolution. In the last part of this eventful century of applied science from, say, 1920 to 1960, there came a second wave: the Second Industrial Revolution. The sign of its arrival was Carothers' production of nylon. Henceforward there was to be deliberate use of scientific thinking directed to the solution of set questions. Individual firms set up research laboratories to make useful discoveries and, indeed, useful discoveries were made. Not many of these were of first-rate originality but each of them contributed its mite of added efficiency or convenience or novelty and hence justified the expense involved by a steady increase in profit. For industry as a whole, the progress year by year was rapid. Each new model of motor-car was faster, safer, more convenient to drive and, in real terms, cheaper than the last. Glass windscreens—to take one example—became first shatter-proof, then clear and transparent, then curved as well. Chemical discoveries led to the development of detergents better than soap and, of course, to plastics and synthetic textile fibres of increasing beauty, utility, durability and strength.

Finally, the development of electronic devices made it possible to build general-purpose digital computers which enabled mental operations to be done automatically and 'mass produced', just as Ford's travelling belt, served by a series of men using power tools—each one designed only for a single restricted operation—had brought mechanical mass-production into operation.

A computer is a machine designed to do a series of operations one after another. The first simple example is the mechanism in a domestic washing machine which can turn on the water, turn it off again when the machine is full, heat it to the desired temperature, agitate the clothes for the required time, stop the agitator and run off the soapy water, run in the rinsing water, run it out again, and then spin the clothes dry. But this example is an over-simplification. Besides doing a series of operations, a computer can be given 'instructions' in such a way that it can make adjustments if unexpected happenings occur. It can, if need be, correct its own mistakes. And because it is operated electronically, it can carry out a prolonged series of steps at very high speed. Hence, by the sophisticated combination of what are essentially a number of basically simple ideas, computers can be built which will not only guide machine tools to do quite complex things but which will as well combine together a series of such operations. In fact, computers are being developed which will 'manage' a factory; besides 'supervising' the different steps of a manufacturing process, the computer can also quite readily be 'programmed' to do the accounts and print and despatch the bills as well.

The narrative of events shows the impact of science exerting its influence at three levels. The first is the intellectual achievement inherent in the discovery of new knowledge. To discover the chemical configuration of indigo, to create a molecule of a compound unknown to nature—Salvarsan, a cure for syphilis—to unlock the secret of electric power: these are triumphs of the human mind. The second level is when abstract knowledge is successfully harnessed to a technical operation. The theoretical relationship between the pressure and volume of gases elucidated by Robert Boyle preceded the development of the steam engine. Faraday's studies of electromagnetism led directly to electric power. The dynamo, the telegraph, the telephone, followed by radio and television are examples of scientific principles applied to practical purpose. In biology, we have already traced the path from Pasteur's studies of fermentation to the eventual conquest of the main infectious diseases by which man and his animals had been plagued since the dawn of history. The list of the practical successes accruing from the application of scientific knowledge to useful purposes is a long one.

The third level arises naturally from the second. The cumulative effect of all the separate technological changes derived from science inevitably began to affect the fabric of life itself. To man the factories, people streamed in from where their small country workshops had been before the new-style industry had put them out of business. The cheaper goods produced by the big steam-driven factories gained markets abroad and more and more workers, this time from farms and homesteads, came into the towns to live in the slums specially built to receive them.

This Industrial Revolution was a revolution indeed. From being a mainly agricultural country, Britain became gradually transformed into an industrial one. The people who had moved from villages, where they formed a part of the social fabric and where their masters, the landlords, had some corporate responsibility for them, became vote-less, rootless cyphers in the new agglomerations of dwellings which were put up round the factories where they worked. And in the towns, they had no gardens or smallholdings to serve as a supplementary source of food and so were entirely dependent on their wages. Often the men who owned the factories had themselves been work-people or were the sons of workmen who had won success, as we should now say, 'the hard way'. As employers, they in their turn drove a hard bargain and paid no more wages than they were compelled to do to get employees.

Yet although the new science and the technology based on it had a great deal to do with the social revolution of the times, the course of events and the interlocking of cause and effect were by no means simple. Science, in the sense in which the term was used a hundred years ago just as it is today, is a mixture of solid practical things and of ideas. The railway trains, that enabled people to travel about and with their families move from remote country districts to the new steam-driven factories, though solid and material objects, were at the same time derived from *ideas*. Although no satisfactory answer can be given to the question of why it was, after thousands of years of human thought, the notion of scientific technology should suddenly emerge in the eighteenth and nineteenth centuries to grow up into the great force we see today, it must be recognised that other kinds of new thinking were on the move at the time science appeared. There was, in fact, a general intellectual eruption.

The most dramatic signs of the coming social change were the ideas of the French Revolution of 1789. The notion that a rigid monarchy, in which a king and a ruling class ruled, and the populace suffered themselves to be so ruled, could be changed and that government should be, as the rebel American settlers put it, by the people for the people, was a new and shocking idea. This idea was independent although parallel with the idea of science. It was generated in France by middle-class professional and business people, mostly living in towns, and the ideas these people developed about abstract freedom and justice and government gradually stirred up the desire of farm workers, who were, in very truth, peasants, to own land and to be given at least some dignity and status. In England in the eighteenth century, on the other hand, life had many pleasant aspects for the majority of people both in town and country. The social distinctions were accepted quite cheerfully and Englishmen, in the main, thought of themselves as being 'free-born Britons', superior to the rest of the world and particularly to the 'frog-eating' Frenchmen. Nevertheless, the new ideas generated by the French Revolution and having little to do with science began to work in their minds too.

Tom Paine, for example, the English Quaker who had settled in America, drank in republican principles and then, returned to England, published the first part of his pamphlet, *The Rights of Man*, in 1791. This, new at the time but common doctrine today, set out the thesis that government is derived from the people, can be changed at their will and should be organised for their benefit. The following year, in the second part of *The Rights of Man*, Paine went the whole hog and asserted that the Monarchy and the House of Lords should be abolished and the country governed solely by elected representatives of the people.

The immediate result of the publication of these ideas was that the Government prosecuted and suppressed *The Rights of Man* and Tom Paine fled for his life to France—where, incidentally, he was almost guillotined for denouncing the Terror! But the longer-term effect was profound. When the results of the ideas of science, manifest as machines and factories and the new crowded industrial towns, collided with the old principles of aristocratic Tory government where workpeople had no rights, political discussion was put down as treason and the combination of workmen to form unions was prosecuted as conspiring—then it was that the new liberal ideas mingled with the new science to change history into what we know today.

Darwin's theory of evolution, the so-called 'survival of the fittest', was one of the great pillars of science supporting the edifice of modern knowledge about the origin of species and showed the story of the Flood and Noah's Ark—previously believed as literal truth—to be a poetic parable. Darwin wrote in his *Autobiography* that the initial idea which stimulated his conception of evolution came from reading Malthus's *Essay on Population*. Malthus's hypothesis was based mainly on intellectual theorising yet to a degree it could be taken as scientific even if it was merely scientific speculation. In the early days of the nineteenth century, the average respectable man, accepting that the prosperity of the cotton-mills, foundries and factories was derived from the new science, sincerely believed that the seemingly scientific ideas of Malthus should be accepted as well. For this reason it was argued that, as a matter of principle, the poor and helpless ought not to be relieved since to do so would interfere with the natural law by which only the 'fittest' were to survive, whereas those unable to win the economic battle were clearly 'un-fit'. It was further believed that Malthus had shown poverty to be inevitable for the majority of mankind on account of the natural increase of population.

No society embraces major changes willingly. The Tory landlords and magistrates in the North of England in 1819 were no more stupid and wicked than are citizens of today. They believed in a system of law and order and good government which the technological changes of the times was making obsolete. On August the 16th of that year a crowd of 60,000 men, women and children, factory workers and their families, unprotected by any legislation to control the conditions under which they were employed and expressly forbidden to combine to protect themselves, gathered in their distress in St Peter's Fields, Manchester. When the magistrates, who had granted permission for the meeting to be held, saw the size of the concourse they took fright. Mounted yeomanry were ordered into the crowd to arrest the speaker —a man called Hunt. Naturally enough, the horsemen were jostled and shouted at by the throng. The magistrates, losing their heads completely, ordered cavalry, standing by in reserve, to charge. The dense mass of human beings, shrieking and cursing, were driven off the field. Eleven people were killed, including two women, a hundred were wounded by the sabres of the yeomanry and several hundred were crushed or injured by horses' hooves. This was Peterloo.

The shock of this monstrous incident gradually showed even the most reactionary and unimaginative that something new was happening to the society of Britain under the influence of the Industrial

Revolution. In 1833, the first effective Factory Act was passed by Parliament, together with the 'children's charter' prohibiting the employment in factories of children under nine years of age (but excluding silk-mills from the prohibition). Between 1844 and 1847 further protection was afforded including the 'Ten hours Bill', limiting the daily hours of women and young people at factories. The laws proscribing Trades Unions as criminal conspiracies had been repealed in 1824 and 1825, largely owing to the efforts of two liberal and hard-working men, Joseph Hume and Francis Place.

As the nineteenth century passed by, the social effect of scientific technology gradually made itself plain. The countries adopting the new principles of applied science, of which Great Britain was the first, soon followed by Germany and then by other European countries and by America, became industrialised. Factories of all sorts sprang up: cotton-mills, engineering works, chemical plants making soap and sulphuric acid and then chemicals of all sorts including the new artificial fertilisers, superphosphate and ammonium sulphate, which began to revolutionise agriculture to keep pace with industry. The social disturbance and the distresses and tensions of trying to apply principles of government evolved to suit a squirearchal rural community to the quite different circumstances of a technological system were slowly and painfully overcome. Social legislation to avoid the more flagrant abuses was gradually introduced.

The Trades Unions, by which the people employed in the factories were to protect themselves, also grew painfully and uncertainly. After they became legal in the 1820s, a series of bitter and often useless strikes supervened in which workpeople were often starved into submission. The savagery with which employers resisted the attacks upon them—as they saw it—of the Unions brought violence, armed attacks and machine-breaking. 'Black-legs' were subjected to terrorism to compel them to conform to the will of the majority. By 1850, however, things had began to improve. The productiveness of industry was enriching the country. The power to vote was being extended. The Trades Unions were becoming more experienced and responsible.

The introduction of science and technology into society produced a steep rise in the population. This was due to two causes. First, when wages were low and conditions bad, children, who could be sent to work at an early age, were an economic advantage. The factories drew them in and very often in truth worked them to death. But perhaps the most potent cause of the increase in population that occurred in the second half of the nineteenth century was the impact of science on public health. People were accustomed to large families, of whom the majority died—as infants, as children or perhaps from pneumonia or consumption (that is, tuberculosis) or from infectious diseases as young men or women. Suddenly all this was changed. The rate of infant mortality began to drop. One infectious disease after another became curable. The expectation of life became longer.

And besides becoming longer, it became better, richer and fuller. It gradually became apparent, first to the better-off and better educated members of the community and later to most of the rest, that fewer children, better fed and clothed and better looked after, were compatible with a happier life. Furthermore, as the decades of the twentieth century succeeded those of the nineteenth and the organised industrial workers, through their Trades Unions, gradually obtained fuller political power, they were able to enjoy the fruits of industrialisation. Today, the cost and trouble of a second or a third child is balanced in people's minds against the cost of a washing-machine or a motor-car.

In considering the way in which the scientific idea became incorporated into the practical affairs of manufacture and hence in the social organisation, one is inevitably struck by the persistence of the strange deviation of the scientific idea propagated by Bentham.

Jeremy Bentham was a curious person who died at the age of eighty-four and whose body, dressed in hat and coat, was placed in a cupboard in University College, London. He was a theoretician and his theory, strangely like science but unlike it in one essential respect, was that every social institution—the law, the system of government, education, economic arrangements, whatever it might be—should be scrutinised on the basis of whether it was likely to provide (in Joseph Priestley's words) 'the greatest good for the greatest number'. Bentham put this idea in another way when he asked (as he frequently did and about all sorts of things) 'What is the use of it?'

Scientific philosophy, like the philosophy of Bentham, challenges preconceived theories, but not on the basis of whether they are 'useful'. Rather the challenge posed by the scientist is 'Is it true?' When this is applied to manufacture, the technologist questions whether the traditional method passed on from the master to his apprentice which claims to be the most effective way of, for example, weaving a piece of cloth, is in fact most effective. He carries out a trial and if a new method does the job better—in some measurable way—he adopts it. The aim of the operation, however, is to make a piece of cloth. When Bentham invented what John Stuart Mill subsequently called 'utilitarianism', he applied the same criterion, not to something with a clear answer—the making of an object, let us say, or the production of a telephone or an electric light—but to human life as a whole. And in life, 'usefulness' is not necessarily the highest aim. Even the term 'good' in the phrase 'the greatest good for the greatest number' may be impossible to define in scientific terms.

Bentham's philosophy exerted a strong influence on the nineteenth century. It brought great benefits but it also brought the ugliness of mass-produced articles and mass-produced houses. It is not easy to assert even now, more than a century after his death, that the main drive of modern societies, which race one with the other to train more and more scientists to be 'useful' in the new science-based industries, where the electronic machines and plastic fibres and all the other goods needed to raise the 'standard of living' are manufactured, is very different from the 'scientific' utilitarianism which was Jeremy Bentham's doctrine.

CHAPTER VIII

A CENTURY OF CITIES

When a community accepts scientific technology as its main philosophy, one of the most remarkable and important results to follow is a growth in the size of its cities and an increase in the proportion of the total number of people in the population that live in cities. Professor Kingsley Davis of the University of California has collected information from various sources which shows that whereas in 1800 only 25 per cent of the population of England and Wales lived in towns of 100,000 people or more, by 1850 the proportion had risen to 50 per cent. It reached 76 per cent by 1900. The rapidity with which the population was becoming urbanised then began to drop off. The proportion in fact only increased by about 3 per cent to 79 per cent by 1925 and remained at about this level for the ensuing twenty-five years.

The same kind of change has occurred in other countries when they in their turn followed the lead taken by Britain and applied science seriously to their affairs. In the United States, it was 1875 before the first 25 per cent of the population came to be living in cities. But after that, the rate of change was very much the same as what it had been in Britain; in fifty years, by 1925, more than half the population were town-dwellers and by 1950 the proportion was 65 per cent and was still rising quickly. Japan, the first Far-Eastern nation to follow the path of technology, increased its proportion of town-dwellers from 22 per cent in 1925 to 60 per cent in 1960. And in the Soviet Union, which by a mighty effort of the national will decided to convert itself from a peasant nation of plains and rivers into an industrial power only in the second decade of the present century, the proportion of the population living in cities, which was 20 per cent in 1930, had become 45 per cent in 1960.

What was the exact cause of this remarkable social change? In the history of mankind, cities first appeared more than 5,000 years ago. Then, they were merely small centres in which a ruler and some of his advisors lived together with a few specialist artificers, while all

116

around the population was rural. For the main, men were concerned with food-gathering and agriculture. And this state of affairs, increasing in complexity and sophistication but nevertheless basically unchanged, continued right up until the modern period of history which we are discussing in this book. Before 1850, no society could be described as predominantly urban. And even the great and ancient cities, such as Rome, Paris or London, were comparatively small in modern eyes.

Only when science and technology had been invented did large cities and the general urbanisation of a nation become possible. To start with, when only horse-drawn waggons were available to transport food into a town, the maximum size of the town was limited by the limited area round about from which supplies could be drawn and the amount of time needed to bring the food in, distribute it and drive the horses and carts out again to fetch the next load. All this was suddenly changed by the steam locomotive of the nineteenth century.

Another factor that brought about the abrupt 'city revolution' in which we—the first civilisation in the history of man ever to do so—are now living, was the effect of scientific thinking on agriculture. Mechanical reapers and binders were among the marvels of science on show in the Great Exhibition of 1851. But equally important was the discovery of artificial fertilisers—ammonium salts, super-phosphate and potash—and the demonstration of their effect by Bennett and Lawes at Harpenden in Hertfordshire in 1842. And at just about the same time, in came the invention of canning as a means of food preservation.

The main factor which limited the size of towns until at last science was used as a way of thinking and from it technology was invented was simply the accumulation of sewage. We have already discussed the reluctance of gentlemen and scholars to apply their educated thoughts to practical affairs. Until they did so, science based on observation and experiment could not exist. Craftsmen and artificers were often highly skilful but they were not educated. It was no accident that technology began in Britain because there it was that the rigidity of aristocratic society was least and nonconformist views on religion as well encouraged a flexibility of mind. Once the productiveness of applied physics and chemistry had been demonstrated, one aspect after another of engineering and manufacture and agriculture and transport was drawn in and educated scientists took over from artisans and mechanics. It was, perhaps, not unexpected that the last practical art to be considered was what to do with sewage. Yet this was a matter of crucial historical importance.

As late as the middle of the nineteenth century, little more than a century ago, pigs were used in Manchester to eat up rubbish and muck that had been thrown into the streets. At the end of the century, the citizens of Paisley defied the town council to remove the hills of ordure in the streets because of the consequent loss of the money paid by farmers for their 'fulzie'. And what of London, the capital city? In 1839, Dr Southwood Smith, physician to the London Fever Hospital, reported to the Home Secretary that 'the masses of the population were crowded in courts and alleys and narrow streets almost insusceptible of ventilation; in dwellings which themselves were often not fit to be inhabited by human beings; while all around the dwellings the utter absence of drainage, the utter omission of scavenging and nuisance prevention; the utter insufficiency of water supply, conduced to such accumulations of animal and vegetable refuse, and to such pondings of odorous liquids, as made one universal atmosphere of filth and stink'.

The problem was a technical one and like all technical questions was, as we have seen, made up partly of a lack of technological knowledge—How were pipes to be made? How could one get rid of sewage even if there *were* pipes and valves and flushing tanks and the like?—but besides the lack of applied scientific thinking, there was also a failure of will. Educated people of ability had so far not applied their minds effectively to the matter. Here is a statement made in 1847 by John Phillips, engineer to the Metropolitan Commission of Sewers.

There are hundreds, I may say thousands, of houses in the metropolis which have no drainage whatever, and the greater part of them have stinking, overflowing cesspools. And there are also hundreds of streets, courts and alleys that have no sewers; and how the drainage and filth are cleared away, and how the miserable inhabitants live in such places, it is hard to tell. In pursuance of my duties from time to time, I have visited very many places where the filth was lying scattered about the rooms, vaults, cellars, areas and yards, so thick and so deep that it was hardly possible to move for it. The effects of effluvia, stench, and poisonous gases constantly evolving from these foul accumulations were apparent in the haggard, wan and swarthy countenances and enfeebled

30: Cottage industry, the spinning of woollen yarn. Employment for a family.
31: Advanced technology applied to weaving. The looms are controlled by punched cards to produce any desired pattern.

32: A man who can make a pair of boots. But the cobbler's productivity was low.
33: A factory in which machines mass-produce boots and shoes. The factory's productivity is high but no man in it can make a pair of boots.

limbs of the poor creatures whom I found residing over and amongst these dens of pollution and wretchedness.*

Under these conditions, barely beyond the memories of people now living, cities could not grow. One of the great social revolutions of mankind, the urbanisation of the populations of the nations, was held back for lack of sewage engineering. Cholera—transmitted by polluted water—made its first appearance among the people of the British Isles in 1831. Between 1848 and 1854, a quarter of a million people died of the disease. In 1868, the death rate from typhoid was 390 per million of the population.

By this date, scientific knowledge of bacteriology and the nature of infectious disease was sufficiently far advanced for it to have begun to influence social behaviour. The connection between sewage and the contamination of the environment in general and drinking water in particular was becoming apparent even to politicians and administrators without scientific training. In 1855, the Metropolitan Board of Works was constituted and Sir Joseph Bazalgette became its chief engineer. He drew up an imaginative scheme for a system of sewers and main drains for London. This included 83 miles of interconnected sewers covering the entire metropolitan area of over 100 square miles to carry away the ordure of the city to an outlet well down the Thames at Barking. For ten years committees and commissions discussed and argued the details of the project. In 1865, the first part of the work was opened by the Prince of Wales, and in 1875 the scheme was at last completed. Only by 1884, however, did the final commission report the success of the scheme in improving the general health of the population.

To make possible the sudden revolution in town-dwelling which mankind elected to adopt for his happiness (if such it be), side by side with the new scientific knowledge of bacteriology and infectious disease and the technological skill and engineering ability of Sir Joseph Bazalgette, it was also necessary to develop a new system of water supply. While the population was scattered in farms and villages and towns were small, the ancient 'natural' practice, followed alike by Abraham and by the Parish of Aldgate, of drawing water from wells sufficed. While cities were small, water could effectively be brought to them in aqueducts, tunnels and troughs along which

* Quoted by Wylie, J.C., *The Wastes of Civilization*. Faber, London, 1959, p. 41.

the flow was conducted by gravity. The New River Company brought water thus in 1613 from springs in Hertford, 20 miles away, to the City of London. The supply pipes through which it was distributed were made of elm trunks, bored out to about 6 inches in diameter. These, though effective enough for their purpose, could not resist much pressure and leaked at the joints. The main advance in public health came from *engineering* developments which made possible the manufacture of cast-iron water pipes; henceforward the drinking water could be kept separate from the sewage and the sewage flushed down the lavatories and kept moving along the sewers.

The growth and development of modern cities were dependent on the ability to produce iron and steel in large quantities: not only for water pipes but for railway lines and the locomotives to run on them and for the steel girders to form the frames of the tall skyscrapers which are the sign and core of all modern cities. Buildings of this kind first appeared in New York. Now they are to be seen, singly or in groups, in every part of the world. The production of iron and steel, upon which the entire development depended, rested on two major scientific discoveries, that of Sir Henry Bessemer in 1856 and that of Sidney Thomas and Percy Gilchrist in 1876.

For many years, iron ore was refined and converted into pig iron in a blast furnace. The chemical principles underlying the operation were, first, the reduction of the iron oxide in the ore to free it from the oxygen combined with it. This was done, in later years, by combusting coke in the furnace to produce carbon monoxide, which in turn took the oxygen from the ore to become carbon dioxide. The second operation was to add limestone to the iron ore and coke in the blast furnace to combine with unwanted silica in the ore and form a glass-like material which would float on the molten iron and be drawn off as slag. A laborious third process then remained to be done, to free the pig iron from its remaining carbon and convert it into wrought iron by 'puddling' it in a reverberatory furnace. It was this process, simple as it would seem in terms of chemistry but complicated and difficult and skilled in technical execution, which the Bessemer converter mechanised. Essentially, his idea was to do the smelting operation in a pot which could be tipped up at the appropriate stage in the process. There is nothing particularly strange to us today in the idea of a needle with its eye at the point end. Yet the notion of putting it there—without which the sewing machine would have been impossible—was a revolutionary intellectual conception. Similarly, Bessemer's idea of a pocket blast furnace capable of being tipped up like a butter churn was equally radical in its day.

But the Bessemer process as it first came into use could not deal with phosphorus; low-phosphorus ores in Europe are rare and costly. There were, however, right up to the end of the nineteenth century, great deposits of iron ore in Lorraine, upon which the continent principally depends for iron and steel today, but which could not be used because no way was known of getting rid of the comparatively large proportion of phosphorus in the ore. Now, in a single year, up to 40 million tons of iron are obtained from these ores. The scientific discovery made by Thomas and Gilchrist was as follows. The sand linings of the Bessemer converter in the course of the process normally produced an acid slag which upset the smelting of high-phosphorus ores and, besides, burned away the vessel; they replaced the sand by alkaline linings such as burnt limestone or dolomite, a basic slag was produced and everything went well. It is upon scientific observations such as this that history and the shape and constitution of modern cities depend.

Their successive changes give the historical growth of modern cities a resemblance to the growth of some sort of living thing. For a city to exist as a unit, it must be possible for the people living in its different parts to be able to move about within it, and while the means of travel were restricted to walking or to horse transport, the geographical size of the city was limited. With the technological development of mechanised systems of transport, the size of cities could increase. There is, therefore, good reason to find that trams were introduced at a certain stage in the 'natural history' of cities in Europe, America and Asia alike.

The first tramway was used, as might perhaps have been expected, in New York, which can claim to be the first of the cities of the technological age. When it was laid down in 1832, the tramcars were drawn by horses at 6 to 7 m.p.h. By 1870, when urban growth was beginning to accelerate, steam power was used to drive the trams. In 1873, cable cars, pulled by an endless wire rope, driven by a steam engine, were introduced in San Francisco; the same system was used on Highgate Hill in London in 1884. Last, and most successful of all, came the electric tram.

And then in the twentieth century came the technological development of the internal-combustion engine. Up to World War I, the cities of industrialised nations were large, to be sure, but they were still only at a first stage brought about by the First Industrial Revolution—the Revolution of Steam. With the advent of the motor-car, cities could grow still further and could become the 'metropolitan conurbations' which they are in our own time and yet the people living in them could move from one margin to the other in about forty minutes' travelling time.

It is interesting to see how the tramcar, from its early appearance in the mid-nineteenth century, gradually spread to the growing cities that emerged all over the world under the pervasive influence of the general atmosphere of applied science. But then the more flexible motor omnibuses, followed by more and more vehicles—lorries, vans and private cars—gradually filled up the streets. The tram, running on fixed rails, began to hamper the free passage of worker bees moving, on their different affairs, from one part of the hive to another. In one city after another, just as they had appeared and covered the arterial channels of communication, so equally gradually the tramway systems withered away.

Then a new change began to appear in the 'natural history' of urban units. In its beginnings, a city was a built-up place with people living all over it. The factories of the nineteenth century were surrounded by the houses of the men and women who worked in them. Soon, however, the managers and more prosperous people moved to a different part of the town to live. Then, just as industrialisation itself and the doctrine of the division of labour made specialisation in work a general condition, so too did parts of the city become specialised. There gradually appeared 'residential areas' where people lived and 'industrial areas' where they worked. As the cities grew in population, the new inhabitants tended to form ever widening rings round the periphery where they were joined—or leapfrogged—by others moving away from the industrial parts in the centre. By this process of urban growth there was produced a city life with its own pulse and circulation. To carry the analogy a stage further, it could be said with truth that the corpuscles of the life blood—the working population who kept the city alive—flowed into the heart of the town in the morning and ebbed back out again in the evening.

The historical development of cities during the last hundred years has been in two directions. First came the attractive pull of factories and, later on, of administrative centres, the head offices of big businesses controlling a number of manufacturing units, local government and specialised organisations such as banks, stock exchanges or exchanges for dealers in metals or grain. The influx of business of all sorts into the cities put up the price of buildings in the central area and thus led to the construction of taller and taller buildings to allow more people to operate in the same small area. The technological advances that allowed skyscrapers to be built demonstrate in a striking way the essential contribution which science made in rendering the modern scene possible. At the same time, it is equally striking to see how the new knowledge and, most particularly of all, the new scientific approach, was only one component with the much older traditional knowledge of the pre-scientific period of history.

We have already touched on the essential role of a plentiful supply of steel to make modern building in city centres feasible. An equally essential development was the appearance of Portland cement.

Cement, that is a substance capable of fixing stones or bricks or any other building material into a solid mass, has been used since the times of remote antiquity. Burnt gypsum and lime were employed for building during the early Egyptian dynasties. The Greeks and Romans used lime, made by burning limestone, mixed with sand. By medieval times, builders were still using lime burned in kilns, often set up near the buildings upon which they were engaged. The lime was mixed with sand and water to make a sort of concrete which, if properly done, would set hard and could be highly durable. Again we find that in the long pre-scientific period from some thousands of years B.C. right up to the eighteenth century the technology of concrete remained virtually unchanged. Then in 1756, John Smeaton, not possessing knowledge of the detailed chemistry involved and ignorant of what today would be called 'solid-state physics', nevertheless, unlike his innumerable predecessors through the centuries, set out, as a man of his peculiar age when the spirit of change was in the air, to experiment to obtain something better. His purpose was to develop the most suitable concrete to withstand conditions of stress and wet for the building of the projected Eddystone lighthouse. His advance was to use a clayey limestone from which to prepare cement in his kilns. This soon led several other builders to start experimenting. In France, L.-J. Vicat made an improved cement by burning a

123

mixture of chalk and clay, ground finely together in a wet mill. Joseph Aspdin in 1824 patented a process for grinding limestone and clay, firing the mixture to convert the limestone to quicklime and then grinding the product finely. His son, William Aspdin, in 1848 set up the first kiln capable of heating the mixture to the high temperature required to make a first-class product and was the first to make available the material now called Portland cement. It was called thus, not because it came from Portland but because it was supposed to look like Portland stone.

This process of events was characteristic of the technology of the First Industrial Revolution. That is, after centuries of accepting traditional ways, suddenly there began questioning, experimentation, trial and a free use of observation and thought. This system of thinking has, of course, continued and developed to our own time. But in the Second Industrial Revolution of the twentieth century, the principles of chemistry are used—consideration of the relative proportions of dicalcium- and tricalcium-silicates, of the amount of tetracalcium-alumino-ferric and of tricalcium-aluminate—together with physical studies using X-ray analysis.

It was only after Portland cement was developed in the mid-nineteenth century that it became possible to build the cities that then began to exist. Concrete itself—so-called 'plain concrete'—has strength to resist compression but not to stand up to tension. In 1868, a French gardener conceived the idea of imbedding a network of iron rods in a mass of concrete. And so, almost accidentally but because he too was imbued with the experimental atmosphere of the times, Joseph Menier invented reinforced concrete to make an ornamental water basin.

As a structural material, reinforced concrete, in which the compression strength of the concrete was now married to the tensile strength of the steel rods which were soon generally used, became indispensable in civil engineering. Architects with reinforced concrete at their disposal acquired a freedom to design buildings otherwise beyond their imagination. Columns, decorations of all sorts as well as structural members, beams and floor slabs allowed the large buildings of the new cities to grow in an infinite diversity and of a size undreamed of before. Bridges and roads, tanks, aqueducts and pipes all could be made out of the new material whose existence only began in 1848.

It is interesting to find that in the 1930s, well into the Second Industrial Revolution, a further major advance took place in the scientific technology of concrete. As I have said, the strength of reinforced concrete is due to the ability of the concrete to resist compression without collapsing and of the steel rods to resist tension without breaking. Just before World War II, Eugene Freyssinet in France conceived the idea that if during the process of setting the concrete it were powerfully compressed while at the same time the steel ties were stretched, the strength of the resulting structure—particularly in its ability to resist bending—would be increased. The result was 'prestressed concrete' made by applying tension to the high-strength steel wire used for reinforcing. The scientific principle—simple when you know it but effective nevertheless—is the same as that involved when one picks up a row of books as a solid 'beam' by applying sufficient pressure to the books at each end of the row. Prestressed concrete allowed the construction of lighter but stronger designs, of leaping single-span bridges and grand concert halls as well as the office buildings, hotels and blocks of flats of today.

The tendency of towns to grow had existed in pre-scientific times but the pace was much slower. In the nineteenth century, the appearance of factories started the spate of migration from the country to the town. The development of railways accelerated this movement by making it possible for the first time for people to move easily from their own localities. The electric telegraph, iron pipes for water, gaslight and then electricity allowed the towns to grow to cities with populations of millions. For a time, their size might have been checked by the difficulties of internal communications, but then came the tramcar, the motor-bus and underground railways. Sherlock Holmes in the 1870s used to get his information to Scotland Yard by sending a telegram from Baker Street. The invention of the telephone then came to allow rapid communication from building to building and the electrically operated passenger lift made travel in a vertical direction as convenient as the tramways and motor omnibuses had made movement in a horizontal direction.

The first phase of the growth of the city was the flowing in of people, as it were from all directions. Then, when a dense central core had become established, the outward flow in one ring after another caused a further steady and continuous growth. The attraction of a big city for manufacturers and traders was the diversity of facilities

125

to be found there. Whatever services and supplies might be needed, they were sure to exist. Similarly, the attraction for the people who lived in cities was, firstly, the diversity of employment—the larger the city, the greater the choice of jobs—and outside working hours, the city could likewise offer every kind of art or amusement and facilities for every interest or activity.

The second phase of city growth—the outward movement of people from the increasingly concentrated and consequently more expensive central core to rings of peripheral suburbs—was not only a movement of people looking for places to live—but of factories as well. A cotton-mill or engineering works of the nineteenth century was characteristically a multi-storey building in which machines were operated by a steam engine. The advance of technology, leading first to mass-production and then to automation, tended to demand a large ground area in which the manufacturing equipment was spaced out in a single-storey edifice. The most recent major change brought about by the development of technology was the added need for extensive parking space in which the operatives' cars could be put while their owners were at work. Thus, while the smaller, more specialised manufacturing units remained near city centres, factories in their turn flowed away in the Second Industrial Revolution to the outer areas.

The change in the character of residential life due to the urbanisation of populations—that is, the sudden revolution from the long pre-scientific period of history when most people lived in the country or in small country towns and villages to the present age when most people live in cities—has had a profound effect on the quality of life. The application of science to produce a steam engine could allow Mr John Jorrocks to live in Great Coram Street, London, one week and hunt in Handley Cross the next while leaving Great Coram Street and Handley Cross not altogether different from what they had been before. Similarly, a telephone or an anti-rabies serum could be used by a man to communicate with a friend or to save himself from the bite of a mad dog without changing the texture of his life. But the steel girders and the prestressed concrete, the sewer pipes and the arterial streets full of motor transport changed in two generations the very context in which life was lived.

To start with, the appearance of cities suddenly changed. Street furniture is an obvious example: the iron sconces with which the link men extinguished their torches before regular street lanterns were available can still be seen where eighteenth- and early nineteenth-century houses survive. Gas-lit street lights of the mid-nineteenth century are a direct contrast to the tall metal or concrete supports for fluorescent strip-lighting of the mid-twentieth century. But a more important city change was the appearance of what has been called the 'cult of the street'.

Many of the older established cities acquired their basic form in the Middle Ages, often around a church or the castle or palace of the principal inhabitant. Frequently the city was surrounded by a wall. Within the wall, the city possessed a form suited to the way of life of the citizens. In Great Britain and in Europe many of the municipalities dismantled their old medieval walls in the eighteenth century and allowed the city to extend and expand. But, except for the main thoroughfares leading to the principal squares and main buildings of the town, the streets were designed for the people who lived in them rather than for those who wished merely to pass through them. It was only when the Industrial Revolution began to gather way, and the populations of the cities began, with a rush, to grow—not with a mixed influx of ladies and gentlemen and artisans, merchants and travellers but with, in the main, a single class of men and women who had come to work in the growing factories and offices—when all this happened, streets began to be built, not as an organic part of a city but merely as rows of dwellings. Here is a passage from a book written by Arnold Bennett in 1904.

The master was in fact coming down the wintry gas-lit street. And the street was Dawes Road, Fulham, in the day of its newness. The master stopped at the gate of a house of two stories with a cellar kitchen. He pushed open the creaking iron device and entered the garden, sixteen feet by four, which was the symbol of the park in which the house would have stood if it had been a mansion. In a stride he walked from one end to the other of the path, which would have been a tree-lined, winding carriage drive had the garden been a park. As he fumbled for his latch-key, he could see the beaming face of the representative of the respectful lower classes [actually, the little servant girl, Sarah] in the cellar kitchen. The door yielded before him as before its rightful lord and he passed into his sacred domestic privacy.*

The rows and rows of small, cheap, undistinguished houses, of

* *A Great Man.* Methuen, London, 1919, p. 41.

which that described was merely one, did not themselves owe anything to science. But they were the product of the scientific thinking out of which the steam power and the gaslight, the trams and the stirring of mass-production came. The first of the streets of back-to-back houses of the mid-nineteenth-century industrial towns, built by the owners of cotton-mills and boiler works before the working people who lived in them had thrown off their voteless helplessness, could be seen to be ugly and damaging to human dignity. The houses of Dawes Road, Fulham, and a thousand other roads like it, which came two generations later had some pretensions to elegance in a limited way, yet their multiplication constituted a new social system part of which has continued to this day. The towns and cities of the eighteenth century, even with their lack of piped water and other technological facilities, possessed an organic unity for their inhabitants. They possessed, in general, a focal centre around which dwelt a diverse community. The new acreages of houses ranged in streets— the so-called 'suburbs'—did not possess within them any central nucleus.

And the city centres themselves quickly changed their character as technology increased its hold. In New York, the towering steel and concrete skyscrapers were of a different order of magnitude from the buildings among which they stood. The occasional relics of earlier times which still remain exemplify this historical metamorphosis in city design. In London, too, the churches, many rebuilt by Wren after the fire in 1666, the spires of which once enriched the skyline, are today lost among the twentieth-century blocks which tower over them just as the parishes of which they were once the centres and the parishioners have also been obliterated.

Paris is an interesting example of the kind of changes which cities have undergone during the short but revolutionary century of the scientific renaissance. Until the year 1853, Paris was a crowded, confused medieval city full of riches and grandeur and squalor all intermingled. Then it was that Georges Eugène, Baron Haussmann, a financier, was appointed Prefect of the Seine and given the task of executing the imperial schemes for the embellishment of the city.

Haussmann showed himself to be a worthy member of the First Industrial Revolution. He installed a splendid new water supply and a gigantic system of sewers. With the new facilities for engineering at his disposal he threw new bridges across the Seine, erected public buildings and cut great streets—the Boulevard de Sebastopol and the Boulevard St Michel—straight through what were then populous districts of the city. Industry had been growing up in Paris and the population had been increasing with it. Haussmann's design was to make an elegant, radial pattern—a beautiful ornament—and by doing so he intended to provide more houses, more space and free movement. Beautiful though the result may have been, it did not fulfil its purpose. The overcrowding of the central area and the congestion of the traffic bears witness to his failure.

The second phase of the science century is apparent in the outer areas of Paris which have become filled in during the last fifty years. Here as in other cities of the age of technology are to be found the large areas of undistinguished dwellings and tawdry shops cut through by great thoroughfares along which the tidal flow of people drive in and out in buses and motor-cars. But fifty years has been too short a historical period for the community of Paris, or of almost any other city, to have been able to solve the problem of providing the environment for a rewarding social life in the face of technological developments such as have never before affected any community in other historical times. The rows of small houses are a by-product of the main technological changes; the towers of concrete flats and the great new highways with fly-over bridges of prestressed concrete are main products of the new technology itself.

The strange change in the behaviour of the human colony, that is the draining away of the population from the countryside and the rural villages and towns into cities which have grown steadily as the century we are reviewing has passed, is something which no pre-scientific historian could have foreseen. The metropolitan cities—New York, London, Tokyo, Paris—have grown continuously into super-cities covering extensive areas of land which previously had been whole counties. Towards their extremities, indeed, these cities in which a major proportion of a nation's population live, are like neither city nor country. The outer suburbs are merely areas of land covered with houses. But while the people who live in these houses are no longer part of a coherent community of citizens, as were their eighteenth-century ancestors, science has come to give them technological advantages for living which these ancestors did not have.

An indirect result of the wealth and employment in factories and offices and the general increase in technology arising from applied science has been the disappearance of domestic service as a paid occupation. But technology has succeeded singularly well in making good the social change it has itself brought about. In the nineteenth century, servants were needed to clean each day the rust and staining of steel table knives. In 1913, Mr Harry Brearley, researching into improved alloys for the manufacture of rifle barrels, prepared a combination of steel and chromium. Its mechanical properties made it unsuitable for rifle barrels but, when discarded, the experimental alloy was found to be resistant to corrosion. Nobody needs a servant to turn the handle of a Victorian knife-cleaning machine today. The blades of the knives are made of stainless steel.

To keep food cool in the pre-scientific household, the servants needed a block of ice, wrapped in a blanket and put in the bottom of an 'ice-box'. But there had died of cholera in 1832 at the age of thirty-six a retired captain of French Engineers, Nicolas Carnot who, almost unrecognised, had made fundamental scientific discoveries about the nature of heat. The only work he published, *Réflexions sur la puissance motrice du feu et sur les machines propres à développer cette puissance*, which came out in 1824, was overlooked for a generation until Lord Kelvin in 1848 drew attention to its immense scientific importance. It was, in fact, the basis of the theory of thermodynamics and made possible the domestic refrigerator—operated by an electric pump to compress a gas and then allow it to expand again—which began to appear in the 1920s.

In the last two or three decades we have seen the conveniences of city life lived within a modern dwelling-unit in a modern technological city proliferate with a rush. A refrigerator is only one of the science-based household machine-tools. Clothes-washing machines and dish-washing machines of considerable sophistication able to carry out automatically a series of operations are a commonplace. The electric iron of my middle-age in the 1960s is demonstrably an object from a different civilisation when I compare it with the flat-iron, one of a pair heated on an open coal fire and slipped into a polished metal shoe before being used, with which the ironing was done when I was a boy. The gas stoves and electric cookers, the indestructible nylon socks which have done away with the need for darning—soon to be followed by curtains, upholstery and carpets of man-made textiles which will do away with the need for dusting—the convenience foods, the silicone polish, the rubber hot-water bottle superseding the breakable, leaking stone one and now, in its turn, being displaced by the electric blanket: all these are products of science and technology which change the very nature of domestic work and life. And latest of all 'essential' pieces of furniture has come the radio and television.

Yet with all this, with all the advantages, comforts and conveniences, with the safety from fire, accident and epidemic disease— in spite of these—it is obvious that the completeness and speed of the social revolution bringing about the urbanisation of the majority of the human population are presenting the present generation of men with new problems. Social restlessness, the discomforts and delays of the daily journeys, the cost of housing bringing tension, overcrowding and often years of endurance of bad conditions, and dull ugliness; all these are signs that the new situation has not yet reached equilibrium. It would be unreasonable to expect so drastic a historical change to have done so in so short a time.

CHAPTER IX

SCIENCE, PLANTS, ANIMALS AND FOOD

During the hundred years from 1850 to 1950 the population of the world doubled. And yet during that time the amount of wheat produced doubled as well. Science may have been the indirect cause of the increase in the numbers of people; it was, however, the direct cause of the twice-times production of wheat. At first, the science of chemistry was brought to bear. In 1842, John Bennett Lawes conceived the notion that the application of specific chemical compounds to the soil would improve crop yield. He invented superphosphate, patented it and set up a factory to make it. He laid out trial plots on his estate at Rothamsted and these plots are still there today, while some of the original experiments are still going on. He observed that by putting down 43 lb of nitrogen per acre in the form of nitrate of soda, the average yield of wheat was increased by 11·9 bushels per acre. If the same amount of nitrogen was added as sulphate of ammonia, the extra wheat yield amounted to 8·1 bushels per acre.

In 1898, Sir William Crookes used these figures in his Presidential Address to the British Association. Just like the British Association Presidents of today, Crookes was concerned about world starvation and what we should now call the 'underdeveloped nations'. Unless the world's supply of wheat could be increased by 1,190 million bushels of wheat in thirty years—that is, by 1928—there would be widespread starvation and distress, he said. The only way to obtain this increase, he considered, was to produce and apply 12 million tons of nitrate of soda a year to 163 million acres of wheat land. He had the genius to foresee that this could only be done if a way could be found to 'fix' the nitrogen gas from the atmosphere.

Twenty-five years after Sir William Crookes spoke, that is in 1913, a team of scientific workers, led by Fritz Haber, at the Badische Anilin und Sodafabrik, did discover a method of producing ammonia by compressing a mixture of nitrogen from the air and hydrogen under immense pressure in the presence of a catalyst, and at a temperature of 500° C. The ammonia produced thus soon became

132

the cheapest form of chemically available nitrogen for industry and agriculture alike. The amounts manufactured by 1928 could supply Sir William Crookes' seemingly fantastic forecast of 12 million tons a year twice over. But by a curious irony of history, the application of *chemical* science, leading to the 'fixation' of nitrogen from the air and the production of nitrogenous fertilisers was not the effective agency by which the vast increase in the world's supplies of wheat was brought about. Even in Great Britain and North-west Europe, where fertilisers are more intensively used on farms than anywhere else, farmers relied more on farmyard manure for their wheat and used the nitrogen-containing fertilisers on their potatoes, sugar beet and mangolds.

The great expansion of wheat production which allowed the growing world population to be fed was due mainly to the science of *biology* and to developments in engineering. Biological science enabled the plant breeders and geneticists to produce new wheat varieties capable of growing in vast, cold and dry areas where no crops could be produced before. And the engineers designed and built the great new machines enabling the crops to be produced and harvested with the minimum of labour. The biologist came into the scene again later on to breed yet newer seed varieties to resist the recurrent attacks of disease fungus.

The early pioneers of wheat-growing in Canada, before the work of Darwin was done and while Mendel and his system of genetics was still unknown, were yet seized with the restless ideas of experimentation upon which science, as we have seen so often before, bases the foundations of material progress. In the 1840s a few grains of wheat were observed to thrive better than their neighbours. From this chance observation, Red Fife was developed. Next, Charles Sanders noticed that one seedling he was testing grew more strongly than the rest. It was soon isolated for seed as Marquis.

This was one more example of the direct approach of the First Industrial Revolution. Progress was achieved more by a bold acceptance of the ideas of trial and experiment rather than by detailed research and deep understanding. Nevertheless, the two varieties— Red Fife and Marquis—proved to be well suited to prairie conditions and enabled wheat to be successfully grown much farther northward and westward than would otherwise have been possible. Then in 1916, when immense fields covering almost the whole area of the plains of Manitoba, Alberta and Saskatchewan were sown with Marquis, there came an epidemic of a fungus disease, 'stem rust'. It was estimated that in that one year alone 100 million bushels of wheat were lost. It soon became clear that the fungus had undergone a genetical change; the principles of evolution had come into play so that the stem rust now established was well suited to its new environment, that is to say, to prairies covered with Marquis wheat. After the epidemic of 1916, there followed others. In 1927, 90 million bushels were lost; in 1935, the loss was 87 million. For the eleven years from 1925 to 1935 the total loss of wheat due to stem rust in Manitoba and Saskatchewan was estimated as nearly 4,000 million bushels.

No preventive treatment was known, no cure could be found. Chemical dips and sprays were unavailing. The bold strokes of the First Industrial Revolution could not avail to solve the problem by a lucky accident. The solution was reached by the methods of the Second Industrial Revolution: fundamental scientific study, hard work and planned experimentation. Plant geneticists and plant pathologists set to work to breed a resistant strain of wheat on sound scientific lines.

It was soon discovered that there were about 130 different races of fungus capable of causing the disease 'leaf rust' and over 200 capable of causing the most destructive of the wheat diseases, called 'stem rust' or 'black rust'. Nevertheless, in 1924 geneticists in the United States succeeded in breeding a wheat resistant to stem rust: it was called Ceres and for a decade until 1935 it was successfully used as the chief immune wheat in Canada. But then a strain of the fungus, *P. graminis*, called by the research workers 'physiological race 56' which could attack Ceres wheat spread across the fields and the crops again succumbed. At once a new wheat strain, genetically designed in the laboratory, was introduced under the name of Thatcher. Thatcher was a double cross of two separate Marquis crosses and was resistant to stem rust 'race 56'. Large areas of the Canadian prairies were sown with Thatcher although it was not resistant to leaf rust, *P. triticina*. Scientists in Canada, however, succeeded in breeding another cross-bred strain of wheat, called Regent; this *was* resistant to the strains of both leaf rust and stem rust current at the time.

In a few years, other strains of rust-producing fungus invaded the wheat fields and again the plant physiologists and geneticists had to

34: The Fleet Ditch in London was until the 1850s an open sewer running under the houses. **35:** A modern sewage works operated on scientific principles. Without installations of this nature, large cities could not exist.

36: Old Istanbul, a city grown up within the circle of a wall.   37: A planned suburb. Separate houses in semi-detachment, not a city (*Aerofilms*).

find seed containing the genes conferring resistance. This is the history of applied science in the field of biology. A basic principle of biology is Darwin's theory of evolution. With the passage of time and the acquisition of new knowledge—by Mendel in 1866, De Vries in 1900 and subsequently in the 1950s and 1960s by the so-called 'molecular biologists' and their studies of DNA—it has come to be recognised that this principle does not stand still. Hence all biological creation tends to evolve and any species of creature—fungus and wheat seeds or the higher animals including man—in its own time may evolve and change the better to suit its environment, by a process in which those better adapted take the place of those less well suited. This is the so-called 'survival of the fittest'. But while the fungi of rust disease, *P. graminis* and *P. triticina*, evolved by the process of natural selection, Ceres and Thatcher and Regent were produced by the intervention of scientific knowledge. It has been largely due to this knowledge that world supplies of wheat have kept up with the ever-increasing human demands of the last hundred years.

The scientific history of wheat-growing in Australia has many similarities to that of Canada and the United States. First came the advance due to the bold application of wit and drive allied to the idea of experimentation. Later on, as in the American continent, came the detailed use of scientific knowledge and patient research. The early Australian settlers used wheat varieties brought from England. These did well in the coastal regions where the rainfall was 22 inches a year or more. Then, as in Canada, the colonists pushed on into the more arid plains of the interior. This time there was no lucky chance finding of Red Fife and Marquis. But chance sent a gifted man, William James Farrer. He was a well-educated Englishman who arrived in Australia in 1870. Although he was a graduate of Cambridge University, he had no special knowledge of science. At the same time, he possessed the enthusiasm and drive of his time and a genius for wheat breeding. He had the insight to see that to suit the climate, a strain of wheat with thinner leaves, to cut down evaporation, and ripening more quickly and with shorter straw than the English varieties was required.

Farrer set to work in 1886 in an improvised laboratory in his house at Lambrigg, New South Wales, using forceps made out of his wife's hairpins and eventually produced what was needed. This was the new wheat, Federation, which was ideally suited to Australian conditions.

Through this application of scientific experimentation the amount of wheat grown in Australia increased from 27 million bushels a year in 1890 to 144 million bushels in 1920. Thereafter, the second phase of the century of science began. In place of bold effort and improvised apparatus there followed laborious study. And as in Canada, the slow, painstaking, systematic efforts of botanists, geneticists and plant pathologists have borne fruit in newer seed varieties able to resist rust and other diseases, produce larger crops or grow in new areas where the rainfall was even more restricted.

The increase in the yield of wheat—and, for that matter, of other crops as well—that accompanied the growth of scientific philosophy was paralleled by a similar increase in the effective production of livestock. The idea of science—the challenging of traditional beliefs and the use of experiment rather than dogmatic assertion to verify argument—started its main spread in the eighteenth century. 'Turnip Townsend' introduced new 'scientific' methods into the farming of his estates in the 1730s and 'Coke of Norfolk' carried out experiments with new crops and new methods—with root crops, rotations and the marling of light land—to such effect that between 1776 and 1816 the rentals of his estates could be raised from £2,200 to £20,000 a year, and yet enable the tenants to make their fortunes.

These advances and improvements and the increase in food which they represented were all part of the spurt forward in thought and enterprise accompanying the general release of new ideas—about politics, economics, even religion, as well as natural science—which were part of the Industrial Revolution. The new industries produced capital and this, in its turn, allowed new things to be done in agriculture. The new-style farmers, Coke and then Robert Bakewell of Leicestershire, besides introducing new farming methods, bred improved cattle. The land in England, now enclosed, partly for technological and partly for political reasons, was no longer cultivated in vast open cornfields where cattle strayed among the stubble in search of food. Instead, the beasts could now be pastured in moderate-sized fields enclosed by hawthorn hedges in which good grass was grown for forage on a sensible rotation. At last, with grass, hay and root-crops available, it was no longer necessary to slaughter cattle wholesale at the end of autumn.

Then a new era for livestock came about as we have seen it did for wheat. In 1809, Albrecht von Thaer devised the first feeding standard for cattle. This was the beginning of the systematic, scientific approach to animal nutrition which later in the century allowed rations of appropriately designed chemical composition to be designed for growth, milk production, the production of wool by sheep and of eggs by hens. Of greater significance still was the occasion in 1840 when Justin von Liebig, then at the height of his fame, delivered his celebrated address to the British Association afterwards published under the title, *Chemistry in its application to agriculture and physiology*. This really founded agricultural chemistry and laid the basis of rational feeding and the use of artificial manures.

Liebig was at that time Professor of Chemistry at Giessen. He was a remarkable man. One of his peculiarities was his flair for making money. He had no snobbish, academic scruples against setting his ideas to work to his pecuniary advantage. He was at one time or another connected with firms for making meat extract, infant foods, invalid foods, baking powder and 'chemical manure'. Just the same, he was a man of high intellectual ability. The effect on scientific thought of his report to the British Association was revolutionary. He completely shattered the old idea that plants derived a large proportion of their organic substance directly from the humus of the soil and showed—what we now know to be fundamental to life on this planet—that the chief if not the sole source of the carbon from which biological substance is built is the inexhaustible supply of carbon dioxide in the atmosphere. Nitrogen he showed was usually absorbed by the roots of plants as ammonia and after having been absorbed was converted into protein. He made it clear that the function of lime was to regulate the soil acidity.

Liebig applied his clear-headed chemical thinking to animal nutrition and physiology as well as to plant growth. In his book, published in an English edition in 1842, he showed the effect of the use of chemical analysis in problems of the feeding of farm livestock. Not only did he make the first accurate analysis of the composition of foodstuffs, he applied the information to the quantitative study of the function of foods.

Hence it came about that in the second half of the nineteenth century, while agriculturalists, not having to kill their beasts in winter, were able to breed livestock systematically for the production of milk and meat and wool and eggs, they could also begin to study the 'feed-efficiency' of the rations which were given to farm animals. And by these means, the production of human food was increased and the efficiency with which it was grown improved steadily, through all the ups and downs of each season's weather.

Liebig's work was the dividing point between the First and the Second Industrial Revolution of applied science. The nineteenth century saw the consolidation of his ideas. In the twentieth century, the discovery of vitamins by Hopkins and Mellanby in England, Steenbock in the United States, Jansen in the Netherlands and many more in the 1920s and 1930s, brought a further stride forward in the effective feeding of farm animals, an improvement in their health and an increase in their rate of growth. In the 1930s and 1940s John Hammond, working at Cambridge, brought about one of the most elegant advances in meat production in this whole scientific history. He studied the way in which meat-animals grow and observed that a lamb, for example, when it is born, is all head, shins and shanks, parts providing little meat and that of poor value. As it grows up, the body first lengthens and then thickens so that the proportion of head and shanks becomes less. In fact, what Hammond saw was that in any animal there are, as it were, tidal waves of growth; the primary one starts at the head and passes backwards, while secondary ones start at the feet and tail. All these waves of growth meet at the loin. Hammond next observed that the composition of an animal—that is the amount of meat on it and whether the meat was tender or stringy and whether there was more or less fat—could be controlled to a considerable extent by the amount of food it was given at different stages of its growth. A rich diet speeded up the waves of growth and a poor one slowed them down. But besides discovering these subtle nutritional effects, the agricultural scientists showed their relationship with genetics.

They found that certain animals responded more to good feeding than others, that is to say, their tidal waves of growth could be varied and controlled more readily to produce exactly the right kind and amount of meat. What the scientific animal husbandmen did, therefore, was to select these animals for breeding. Thus while 'unimproved' animals—of which the wild boar is the archetype—grow up with little change in the proportional development of loin to head, or fat to bone, the genetically 'improved' breeds change greatly in these respects as they grow up.

138

During the hundred years or so from 1850, the application of the scientific attack and of scientific knowledge to the production of food has led to a series of signal advances. Chemistry applied to fertilisers we have already discussed. The alternative use of chemical science was to avoid losses of crops, first by the use of Paris Green and Bordeaux Mixture—compounds of arsenic and copper—in 1870 and 1885 to destroy insect pests, followed two generations later by more sophisticated compounds. DDT was one of the most effective and widely used to destroy numerous types of caterpillars, beetles and flies. Later still, bringing the story up to the middle of the present century, came a group of so-called chlorinated hydrocarbons and organic phosphorus compounds.

Following chemical agents designed to kill insect predators, came the development of selective weedkillers. These have exerted a very material influence on the supply of human food. For example, by 1950 it was estimated that from 5 to 10 million acres of cereal farm-land in Canada was treated with the compound 2,4-dichloro-phenoxy-acetic acid to keep wheat free from weeds.

The predominant role of biology—the use of genetics to produce improved seeds and improved livestock—has also been described. A different application of biological science was the development of canning as a major means of preserving food and allowing it to be transported and distributed to countries far distant from its place of origin. The scientific principle upon which canning depends is, first, the understanding that the principal reason that foods decay and go bad is the presence in them of living micro-organisms; second, that these micro-organisms can be destroyed if the temperature is raised to a high enough level; and third, that when the micro-organisms have been killed by heat the foods will keep for long periods of time provided they are wrapped in an impervious covering—of which a tin can is the commonest—so that no other micro-organisms can gain access to them.

Other technological means of increasing food by preventing loss from decay have been to dry it by mechanical means so that—in dried egg and dried milk, dehydrated fish and meat and potato powder and peas—the moisture content is too low to allow decay-producing micro-organisms to grow. The use of mechanical freezers—a further technological advance—can also be looked at as a type of dehydration. The low temperature slows up the metabolic processes of the micro-organisms, to be sure, but it also removes the moisture from circulation by turning it into ice crystals.

Although the development of machinery freezing and dehydrating foods—great spray-driers and blast-freezing equipment and the like—contributed to the steady increase in the efficiency of food production during the century from 1850, more important still was the construction of more and more sophisticated power-driven agricultural machines. Between 1830 and 1850, stationary steam engines were used on some English estates to draw large multiple-furrow ploughs backwards and forwards across a field by means of cables and in some instances steam-driven threshing machines were used as well. Cast iron and steel plough-shares were introduced at about this time and, in parallel with the upsurge of mechanical inventiveness in manufacture, a number of important inventions were made in farm machinery. Among these were several patents taken out early in the 1830s for mowing machines for cutting hay or corn based on the principle of a row of triangular reciprocating knives passing backwards and forwards across a series of fixed fingers or guards. This principle is used to this day. McCormick, one of the patentees, has been said to have 'straightened the bent backs of toilers' all across the world. The increase in effectiveness of a man with such a mowing machine compared with his performance using a scythe was prodigious.

The idea of improvement and invention, not science but using machines and technologies arising from a few basic applications of science, quickly grew and increased in agriculture. By 1870, advances in wheat growing and soil management could bring their full benefit as a result of a piece of applied ingenuity. This was a device for tying a piece of twine round a bundle of cut corn. With the development of the Locke harvester—the first effective reaper and binder—an end of the tedious and wasteful process of binding sheaves by hand was in sight. About 1878 the remarkable device called the 'Appleby knotter' appeared which was used almost unchanged for the following eighty years. Between 1870 and the end of the nineteenth century a host of new agricultural machines came into use. There were manure spreaders, seed drills, disc ploughs and harrows, cultivators and in America devices for sowing and for harvesting the great fields of maize grown in the corn belt.

But the main revolution in rural industry, as in urban life, was brought about by the mixture of science, technology and general inventiveness of the internal combustion engine. After their thousands of years' use by farmers, the population of horses—slow, hungry, susceptible to disease and ill-temper—withered and dwindled with the coming of the twentieth century. In place of horses came the tireless, versatile and far more powerful and amenable motor tractor. Of all applications of science, this brought about the greatest increase in the ability of one man to produce food. In the United States in 1910 about 4,000 tractors were built; in 1941, the number built was nearly 400,000 and about 2 million were in use. The same rapid increase in mechanisation took place—sometimes a little later, to be sure—in Great Britain, Germany, France, the Soviet Union and in every country into which technology spread. It was calculated by the U.S. Department of Agriculture that whereas in 1830 it took fifty-eight man-hours of work—ploughing, sowing, harvesting and thresh-ing—to produce twenty bushels of wheat, by 1896 this figure had been reduced to nine man-hours mainly due to the introduction of the reaper and binder and to the use of mechanical threshing. By 1940, however, the amount of human labour had again been halved; with the availability of tractors, the twenty bushels of wheat could be obtained for the expenditure of only four man-hours of labour.

The historically abrupt introduction of power machinery into agri-culture has produced—silently and largely unnoticed by the general population of the countries in which it has happened—an extra-ordinary effect on the productivity of food producers. Besides multi-plying the effectiveness of human labour by fifteen times, the techno-logical devices I have been writing about have made the labour more effective. A peasant hoeing land by hand or dragging a plough along with a rope over his own shoulders could only make an inferior seed-bed for all his efforts. Even when a farmer had an ox or a team of horses there were heavy, difficult types of land which defeated him. With a tractor pulling a plough with a steel mouldboard of proper design he could not only prepare the soil quicker but better and deeper as well. Mechanical harrows, accurately designed seed-drills and tools for cultivation all allowed land to be more effectively used. The harvesting machinery of a generation ago allowed more of the crop to be collected, cleaned and stored than was previously possible. And the historical trend is far from spent. Hay-making as portrayed in romantic paintings was always a wasteful process. Even if the crop was not spoiled by rain, to grow hay to its 'ripe' stage was to allow the feed value—highest when the leaves of the grasses are still green—to deteriorate as the stalks grow stronger, and hence tougher and less digestible, and the content of vitamin A-activity to wither in the sun. Modern machinery allows the crop to be harvested young and processed as dried grass or converted into silage. Again, modern combine-harvesters, besides saving the labour of cutting, binding up the sheaves, stooking, carting, stacking and threshing, also allow the crop to be garnered exactly at the right time and recovered without loss.

To feed 5 million working adults in the United States in 1840, 4 million people had to work on farms. To feed 30 million in 1900, only 10 million had to work at agriculture. But to feed 50 million in 1942, the very same number as had been required in 1900 for the total nation of 30 million workers—that is 10 million—still sufficed.

All this historical evidence implies that the annual world supply of human food has continuously and to an accelerating degree increased during the past century due, like so much else, to the application of science and technology to its production. It is not easy to assess by how much each year supplies of food have increased. The degree of industrialisation has not been uniform in the different countries of the world and while many of the great food-producing territories are fully industrialised—Canada, the United States, Australia and more recently Russia—there are other areas, for example parts of South America and India, where the history of industrialisation is in its early stages and vastly more food could be grown. Nevertheless, one authority, Woytinski, in a great study entitled, *World Population and Production Trends and Outlook*, published in 1953, estimated that since 1850, when technological machines and scientific discoveries first began to be seriously applied, the increase in food production has been more rapid than the increase in population. For the middle decades of the twentieth century, the U.S. Department of State has estimated that whereas the total number of people in the world was growing at the rate of 1·7 per cent each year, the amount of food produced each year was increasing by 3 per cent. The people who made these estimates were concerned with the practical day-to-day business of trade. For them the history of past years was important as a means, not of pleasure or scholarship, but of forecasting the future. And they forecast that by 1975 there would be a 'surplus' each

38: Hand reaping on a farm worked by the family that owns it. 39: The combine-harvester is a happy marriage of farming and technology.

40: The intensive production of veal. Food technology becomes 'agribusiness' (*Farmer and Stockbreeder*).

41: The use of science and technology to destroy crop pests and ensure the efficient production of food (*Farmer and Stockbreeder*).   42: The irrigation of crops for which an appropriate supply of water needs to be allocated (*Farmer and Stockbreeder*).

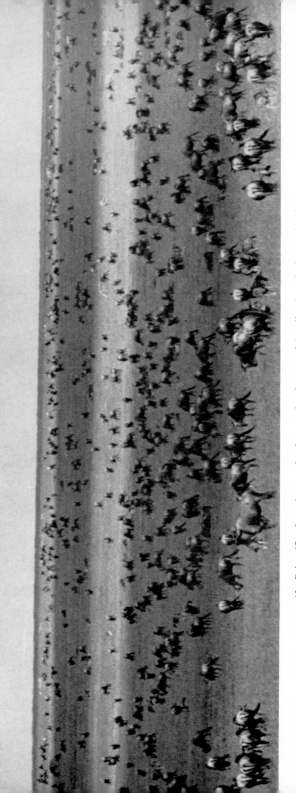

43: Scientific thought can lead to technology and 'agribusiness'. Or, as in the photograph, some land can most efficiently be employed in raising game.

year of 40 million tons of wheat and 70 million tons of rice which farmers would not be able to sell. If in the ten years preceding 1975, scientific means were discovered to increase crop yields per acre—a likely happening—the surpluses could be bigger still.

The human race, in spite of man's superior intellect and the several thousand years of civilisation, is, from one point of view, merely one of the world's animal species and is equally as subject to the principles of biology as any other creature. One of the basic biological principles is that when the environment in which a colony of living organisms is subsisting becomes favourable to that species, its numbers increase. For example, when a few yeast cells are put into a flask of broth, they multiply and their numbers grow at an accelerating rate until, when the environment in the flask begins to become congested, the rate of increase becomes slower and eventually stops. Similarly, a colony of white rats will reach an equilibrium. Or again, rabbits, finding themselves for the first time in Australia, or Pilgrim Fathers arriving in America, increase in numbers as long as the environment—the land and the climate, the supply of food and water, and the absence of too many hostile Red Indians or germs of myxomatosis—allows. In the history of the century from the 1850s to the 1950s, several factors in the human environment became markedly more favourable than they had been before. In general, these were, firstly, the enormous increase in industrial and agricultural productivity—that is to say, in wealth—and, secondly, the defeat of the germs of infectious disease.

Scholars have estimated that after hundreds of thousands of years of slow increase, the number of human beings in the world reached about 250 million at around the beginning of the Christian era. Then, as the slow improvement of civilisation spread through the species, the numbers rose, to 500 million by 1650. The increase, at a slow rate of compound interest, went on and in a further two centuries, that is by 1850 at the beginning of the period of history which we are considering, numbers reached 1,000 million. Then as the century of applied science began things changed. Instead of a growth of population of 2 to 3 million extra people a year, the rate jumped up to 12 to 13 million a year and the world's population reached 2,000 million in 80 years, that is by 1930.

History is the account of times past. Yet, even remembering the dictum that 'all that men learn from history is that men learn nothing from history', it is not unreasonable to reflect on the implications of

143

the increase in world population during the past century. If the rate of the past eighty years is maintained until 1975, total numbers will reach 4,000 million, as well they may. But there is no sense in using the mechanics of arithmetic in place of thoughtful observation and an understanding of the biological growth of animal populations. People are lacking in judgement and a grasp of the science of biology alike when they use the arithmetic of the present annual rate of increase of the human population to forecast that in 600 years, that is by A.D. 2550 or thereabouts, the entire dry-land area of the globe will be covered by men, women and children standing with their arms straight down by their sides, shoulder to shoulder as at a football match. No biological species and least of all mankind with all its subtle social behaviour and intellectual foresight behaves thus. Increases in numbers continue to a time when the curve reaches a point of inflection, the rate slows down and an equilibrium is attained.

The present period of history is undoubtedly a period of rapid population growth. We have already discussed the factors which have led to the remarkable urbanisation of nations in almost every part of the world. The great super-metropolitan cities are certainly crowded areas. The high-density band from Boston to Washington D.C. in the United States has an area of 14,000 square miles, an aggregate population of over 28 million people—over 2,000 people per square mile—and very limited natural resources. The Greater London area, the territory of Greater Tokyo, Holland, Belgium, even Hong Kong, which barely trades with its hinterland but houses more than 3 million people on 389 square miles—that is almost 8,000 people per square mile—all these are signs of the world's population growth yet all are thriving areas supporting the evidence that the complex technology of the period does indeed enable communities to live in towns and yet at the same time increase production of food from the land.

If the history of the past century teaches us anything it is that the operations of Nature as elucidated by scientific investigation are something more than intellectually satisfying systems of thought—like rules of grammar or the moves of a game of chess. The so-called 'laws of science', if they are worthy of the name, do explain reality. By applying them to mechanical things, mankind has produced automobiles and aeroplanes, drugs and vitamins, fertilisers and combine-harvesters. One of the results of all these separate developments which have made civilised life safer and more comfortable has been an

144

increase in human numbers. Using knowledge of the immediate past to try to foresee the immediate future, there is little to imply that population numbers are outrunning their food supplies.

One of the reasons for man's ability to colonise practically the whole of the world's land surfaces has been his adaptability in matters of food. His omnivorous nature and his intelligence and forethought—culminating in the last century's development of food science and technology—have enabled him to withstand seasonal shortages and even serious failures of his crops. Nothing, not even modern science, has protected him from the *fear* of famine, from which many people suffer today, or from its reality. History is full of references to famines right up to the present day. Hesiod described famine in 700 B.C.; Herodotus writes of it in 450 B.C. 'Give thy son, that we may eat him today, and we will eat my son tomorrow,' says the author of the Second Book of Kings, vi, 28. The Chronicle of Novgorod, written between A.D. 1016 and 1471, refers often to hard times. 'This year it was cruel . . . the people ate lime tree leaves, birch bark, pounded wood pulp mixed with husks and straw; some ate buttercups, moss, horse flesh; and thus many dropping down from hunger, their corpses were in the streets, in the market place, and on the roads, and everywhere.'

The registers of the Parish of Greystoke, in the Cumberland Hills in England, during the year 1623 show that some forty people died of starvation. On September the 11th Leonard, son of Anthony Cowlman of Johnbie in that parish was buried, 'which child died for want of food'. The next day Jaine, his mother, a widow, was buried also; she 'died in Edward Dawson's barn at Greystoke for want of maintenance'. Then on September the 27th and October the 4th, John Lancaster, another child, and his mother Agnes were buried too, deserted by the father; they also 'died for want of food and means'. So here in rich civilised countries we find accounts of famine in the times long before the scientific revolution came to its full force in the nineteenth century and brought the sharp increase in population which we have been discussing.

There are two reasons why many people believe, in face of the historical evidence, that the mid-twentieth century is a period of human starvation. In 1623, even within a small country like England, few of the parishioners of Greystoke will have known that homeless people were dying of hunger in barns and to those 20 miles away the

145

doings of Greystoke will have seemed as remote as happenings in Thule seem to us—even more so, because a journalist in Manchester can ring up Alaska on the telephone if he wants to. Technology once again has changed human history by the invention of world-wide instantaneous communication. A child starving anywhere in the United Kingdom is 'news', although many more starved before than after the unfinished technological revolution of 1850–1950. Communications from one part to another of the countries represented by the United Nations are now almost as efficient as between counties of the United Kingdom so that modern peoples can be told the estimated numbers of children not getting enough to eat.

A second reason why these numbers mislead those who hear them is because scientific knowledge of nutrition has become complex and detailed. Man is physiologically adaptable in matters of food. To do a certain job, when an unrestricted supply of food is available, a man may use 1,700 calories as the 'basal' supply of energy to keep a body weighing 150 lb running smoothly; and for his day's physical work he will use another 1,300 calories, making 3,000 in all. If food becomes scarce, however, so that he can only obtain enough to supply 2,500 calories, he will come to no dire harm, even if he still has to do 1,300 calories-worth of work. His physiological adaptability will come to the rescue. He will gradually lose, say, 10 lb in weight and his 'basal' needs will come down to 1,200 calories. He will be thinner and a whit less efficient, perhaps, but many a poet and many a philosopher have lived to old age thus. Yet all of these, and all those eating any less than the target assessment of 'optimum' amounts of vitamin A and a dozen other vitamins and mineral substances and proteins will appear on the lists to swell the statistics of those calculated to be undernourished in the world.

When we say that the century of science has radically affected the growth of crops and the husbandry of animals, and when we then reflect that these changes together with the invention of technology have led to a doubling of the human population and an alteration in the distribution of that population from a scattered covering of the land into a gathering together, as it were, into a few large swarms clustering in the great urbanised conglomerations of modern civilisation—when we say all this, what is implied is that by using scientific thinking mankind has affected the total ecology of the world. Ecology is the study of living creatures in their environment; it is what is

146

popularly called 'the balance of nature'. All farming operations have an ecological effect. The farmer tips the balance of a 50-acre field over in favour of wheat and into an unfavourable state for 'weeds'. A poultry farmer will tip the balance towards an improved environment for chickens rather than for foxes.

Although before the mid-nineteenth century, agriculture and the building of cities and roads, the draining of marshes and the subduing of wolves had had significant effects on quite large areas of the world, nevertheless outside these 'garden' territories lay even vaster areas of wild land and untamed sea where man had no dominion at all and Nature ruled unchallenged. Now, after a century of science, although there are still large areas in north-eastern Russia where settlement by man is still resisted by ticks—disease-bearing insects—and the rain forests of the Congo are still inhabited only by pygmies practising a pre-scientific social life, in the main, the whole of the earth is now subject to man. And just as urbanisation and overcrowding and mechanised war, all science-based phenomena, arose in their present form by accident and without being planned as such by scientists or anybody else, so too have a number of ecological changes, also due to man's technical intervention, occurred by surprise rather than by intent.

In 1930, the farmers in Uganda grew their cotton in small individual plots. With the introduction of modern technology, these became larger and larger and soon merged together into great cotton-growing estates. Other farms developed as well and it became necessary to shoot the lions that came out of the forests to prevent them from eating the farm livestock. But growing wealth and the increasing use of science did not cause the administrators of the century to overlook the well-being of the indigenous farmer. And soon Game Reserves were established in order to tidy up the situation. If science could be applied to the production of food and cotton and the proper management of tame animals for the use of man on one side of the fence, why should not the same knowledge be applied to the management of wild animals on the other side?

The history of what happened teaches a lesson in humility. The original idea—that all that needed doing to preserve wild life was to set aside an area where the animals would not be harried or shot and thereafter all would go on as before—was quickly found to be too naïve and simple. It had been pointed out by Fraser Darling that wildfire has been natural in Africa throughout the ages, changing the forests of the plateaux into savannas and diversifying the grasslands and open glades. The many hoofed animals and their predators are well adapted to these fires and simply move on when they come. However, in order to avoid undue danger and destruction, any burning at all in the Game Reserves was absolutely forbidden. As a result, a rank growth of uneatable grasses caused the disappearance of many of the animals for whose benefit the new arrangement had been made. But another result of the simple well-meant policy of inviolacy was even more unexpected: this was a plague of hippopotamuses.

Before the application of scientific methods to the area, the hippotamuses for which the Queen Elizabeth National Park was particularly noted were kept in check by the local inhabitants who killed those they needed for meat and hides. When this was stopped and their chief predator consequently neutralised—quite apart from the lions, more of which were shot than before to keep them from attacking the cattle—the hippopotamuses started to multiply. Where there were hundreds before, there were soon thousands. Nightly they scoured the countryside for miles around grazing and searching for more grass. In a short time, in place of a parkland of scattered trees and bush grazing, there was bare ground and a greatly increasing growth of profitless thorn scrub.

This is but one example of the ecological effects of the spread of applied science. Because of advanced technological processes applied to cotton growing and cattle farming in this one part of Africa, a plague of hippopotamuses blighted large areas of the land. Similarly it was lack of ecological insight in 1944 that brought the Tanganyika ground-nut scheme to disaster. This was a great operation to clear large areas of forest and bush using heavy mechanical gear and modern earth-cultivating machinery. But when, after tremendous effort and the investment of very large sums of money, the bush and scrub were cleared away, the anticipated crops of ground-nuts—to provide margarine and cattle cake and, so it was hoped, a synthetic 'wool' fibre as well, called Ardil—did not grow.

Ecology is the branch of the science of biology which deals with the relationship between living things and the whole of their environment both living and non-living. The power and command over nature which the century of science gives to the men of the mid-twentieth century inevitably tips the ecological balance. Not only are the growth of crops, the development of food animals, the change in the nature of land—from scrub to farm-land, or to desert—the effect of technological changes on wild animals all ecological happenings. Man himself is also involved.

Between November 1964 and November 1975 the Aswan High Dam will cause the waters of the Nile to rise 200 feet above the highest level to which they have ever risen before. Gradually, a great lake will be formed, 300 miles long and 16 miles wide. The rocks of Nubia, the temples and monuments, the wall paintings, the ancient forts and the modern villages where people live will be inundated. And the human ecology of this strange people, who were not subject to the Ethiopians but lived under their own kings when Strabo saw them 2,000 years ago, will be disrupted. The first 100,000 were evacuated in 1962.

The Nubians will not be sacrificed for nothing. The High Dam, to be one of the great technological triumphs of the age, is projected to bring water and electricity and wealth to the land of Egypt. And the transplantation of the nation of Nubia is merely a part of the ecological change which has increased the yield of crops and animals for food, enlarged the numbers of the human race and drawn them together in the space of a short hundred years into town areas where most of them now live.

This is not an entirely comfortable period of history to live in. It is seldom so in any revolution nor can it be agreeable to find oneself dwelling on the slopes of a volcano in eruption. The eruption of science as a way of thinking has indeed produced a continuous and increasing 'lava-flow' of material and social changes. We are presented with a challenge—to keep our heads and control the ideas for which these very heads are responsible.

There are in the world large numbers of people living in misery and squalor. Some of these are to be found in so-called 'underdeveloped' countries, others are to be found among the migrant groups of American citizens, agricultural labourers who move from place to place following the harvest; and America is the richest country on earth. Others are our own neighbours, if we but knew it.

'Hard cases make bad law', as the saying goes, and lazy thinking, easily overwhelmed by the dynamism of the times, equips man poorly to assess the situation which it is his business to control. Before, therefore, we decide whether the facts call for pessimism or optimism let us consider the work of Seebohm Rowntree. He achieved the astonishing performance of carrying out three social surveys among working-class families in the city of York. The first was done in 1899, the second in 1936 and the third in 1950. Rowntree conceived the idea of a 'poverty line'. This was the weekly sum of money available to a family comprising a man, his wife and three children, any less than which made it impossible for them to obtain an adequate diet no matter how much nutritional knowledge or dietetic ingenuity they possessed. In 1899, 71 per cent of the working-class population of York was malnourished according to the harsh logic of the 'poverty line'. By 1936 the figure was 31 per cent, amounting to 17,185 souls; and by 1950, the proportion was less than 2 per cent and the number 1,746. Properly applied, science brings wealth and wealth health.

44: The goal of history.   45: Science and technology bring wealth and knowledge so that a community can build a good society.

46: Citizens in the Science Century. Victoria Station, London, any working day.

CHAPTER X

THOUGHT, FEELING AND BELIEF

Although the roots of modern science can be claimed to have begun their growth in the seventeenth century when great men, of whom Newton, Galileo and Boyle are shining examples, were doing their work and the Royal Society was founded, there is good reason for taking the middle of the nineteenth century as a starting point for the remarkable period of social change derived from science, the several different aspects of whose history we have been considering. From 1778 until 1820, for a period of forty-two years, Sir Joseph Banks had been President of the Royal Society. Under his autocratic rule, the Society lost its vigour and its Fellows, many of whom were not scientists at all, became lethargic and insensitive to the implications of the new knowledge. But although educated men in general and many scientists as well were blind to the power of scientific insight, there were others who foresaw its importance. Largely as a revolt against the dilettante state of the Royal Society, a number of these formed the British Association for the Advancement of Science in 1831.

The idea behind the British Association was derived in rather a curious way from Germany. In 1822, a German scientist, Lorenz Oken, had the notion of calling together in Leipzig a group of men interested in medicine and natural science. A number of the petty rulers of the German states at the time were highly suspicious—just as modern governments today fight shy of 'peace congresses'—and only thirty-two philosophers were bold enough to attend what was the first European scientific conference ever to be held. Nevertheless, further meetings took place in succeeding years in different German towns and by 1828, when von Humboldt was president and the conference was held in Berlin, the King of Prussia attended as a guest. Science had become respectable and a matter of public interest—at least in Germany.

But another guest at the Berlin conference, and one of more importance to British science, had been Charles Babbage. Babbage was a remarkable man, a mathematician, holder of the Lucasian Professorship of Mathematics at Cambridge, he was as well an enthusiast. For example, he found that many of the standard tables used by mariners to calculate their position at sea were full of mistakes. From time to time the Admiralty issued tables of corrections. Babbage looked into these and before long the Admiralty found it necessary to distribute tables of corrections to correct the earlier tables of corrections. Seeing that computation, which at that time had to be done laboriously by clerks hired for the purpose, was an unreliable process no matter how meticulously the work was checked, he set himself to devise a 'calculating engine'. This was an extraordinary machine and, in fact, has been the basis of the modern digital computers which were developed a century later and upon which automation, one of the major historical events of the twentieth century, was based.

Babbage came home from Berlin immensely impressed with what he had seen and heard and, with his quick insight, convinced of the significance and importance of science in the affairs of the community. He wrote an enthusiastic account of what he had witnessed in Germany in the *Edinburgh Journal*. This came out in 1829 and made a considerable stir. Its good reception encouraged Babbage to write a book, characteristically entitled, *Observations on the Decline of Science in England*, in which he attacked the sleepy hauteur of the Royal Society, the blindness of a largely classically-educated Parliament and the sheer stupidity of society at large. In a long and favourable review of Babbage's book, Sir David Brewster, a distinguished Scottish physicist, called on the 'nobility, gentry, clergy and philosophers' to combine together to support an organisation similar to that in Germany. The following year, 1831, the first meeting of the British Association was held in York. It can almost be said that Charles Babbage holds the distinction of having played a part in the first wave of applied science which changed the whole flavour of civilised life in the 1850s and also, by way of the electronic computers born from his calculating engine, made a significant contribution to a major further change a century later.

But although the material contributions of science to practical affairs advanced at a gallop, as the earlier chapters of this book have set out to show, the idea of science itself was only reluctantly accepted by the leaders of nineteenth-century thought. Dickens reflects the contempt that citizens of 1837, sure of the accepted values of their times, felt for science and the mockery that unimaginative people, comprising the majority of the population, poured on scientists.

> May 12, 1827, [wrote Dickens] Joseph Smiggers, Esq., P.V.P.M.P.C. presiding. The following resolutions unanimously agreed to: 'That this Association has heard read, with feelings of unmingled satisfaction and unqualified approval, the paper communicated by Samuel Pickwick, Esq., G.C.M.P.C., entitled "Speculations on the Source of the Hampstead Ponds, with some Observations on the Theory of Tittlebats", and that this Association does hereby return its warmest thanks to the said Samuel Pickwick, Esq., G.C.M.P.C. for the same. That while the Association is deeply sensible of the advantages which must accrue to science from the production to which they have just adverted—no less than from the unwearied researches of Samuel Pickwick, Esq., G.C.M.P.C., in Hornsey, Highgate, Brixton and Camberwell—they cannot but entertain a lively sense of the inestimable benefits which must inevitably result from carrying the speculations of that learned man into a wider field. . . .*

Although the mockery of the 1830s continued for a generation— even Bishop Wilberforce attempted to overbear T. H. Huxley's account of Darwin's theory of evolution at the meeting of the British Association held in Oxford in 1860 by jeeringly asking him whether he claimed to be descended from a monkey on his father's or his mother's side—the denigration had gradually been dwindling. University College, London, had been founded in 1826, primarily as a revolt against the Test Acts which decreed that members of the Universities of Oxford and Cambridge must subscribe to the Anglican Communion. Although established in the cause of religious liberty, it provided scientific studies as a basic part of its teachings. Then in 1851, Owens' College was set up in Manchester.

It was natural that the people in the North of England should be among the first to see that the idea of science was the most important intellectual conception of the age. They were situated in the middle of the material products of technology. It was there that the great steam engines were made and the factories most obviously dominated the landscape and most directly affected people's lives. Hence, when John Owens, a wealthy merchant, left nearly £100,000 to found a college, leading men, men of imagination and drive, were there to take up the idea. The college was opened in the old house of John Cobden and from it sprang the modern Manchester University.

* *Pickwick Papers.* Nelson, London Classics, p. 1.

But even by 1851, the year of the Great Exhibition, although civilised people were beginning to marvel at what science could do, the realisation that it was growing into a major philosophy and guide of social behaviour had still only been appreciated by few. The Prince Consort, the driving force behind the Great Exhibition, had some idea of what was happening. Tyndall, a distinguished chemist, realised that Pasteur's germ theory of infectious disease must inevitably change the ideas of intelligent and devout men about such notions as that epidemics were sent to punish cities for the sins of their inhabitants. The logic and usefulness of such devotional activities as praying for the recovery of sick people rather than treating them with vaccines was also questioned by Tyndall. The scientific idea of the *ascent* of man from the lower animals by a process of evolution rather than his *descent* from the angels had already led to painful rethinking by serious-minded people following Huxley's address in 1860 to which I have already referred.

And so, starting with a small Government grant in 1852, to set up a sickly Science and Art Department, gradually Britain, like other civilised nations, began to undertake science as a matter of national importance. But in spite of the palpable impact of science on the human scene it was late in the nineteenth century before science was recognised generally as being something which affected man's behaviour rather than simply ministering to his comforts. The British Association battered away. In 1855, a committee presented a report on 'whether any means could be adopted by the government or parliament that would improve the position of science or its cultivators in (the) country'. In 1872, a request that the Government support the Meteorological Office was unsuccessful. 'I am in principle opposed to all the grants and it is my intention not to entertain any applications of this nature,' said the responsible Minister in turning down an application—for £300 a year!

The importance of the scientific idea was gradually being recognised nevertheless. In America, the Massachusetts Institute of Technology was founded in 1865. The Zurich Polytechnic was in 1873 well established and was exciting great admiration throughout Europe. In Germany, the Physikalisch-Technische Reichsanstalt was set up in 1887 under the direction of Helmholz. Then in 1896, after one more outburst of agitation by the British Association, supported now by the Royal Society, the decision was taken to create a National

Physical Laboratory. At first, the official aim was a limited one for 'a public institution for standardising and verifying instruments, for testing materials and for the determination of physical constants'. This was a good deal less than the vision of the British Association for an establishment 'limited by no speciality of aim, nor by the demands of the commercial world . . . invested with all the dignity and permanence of a national institution, a physical laboratory aiming at the highest. . . .'

The establishment of the National Physical Laboratory in 1896 was more of a sign of what was to come than a reality. But it was, nevertheless, a cloud as big as a man's hand in the firmament of social ideas, presaging bigger things. It started with two groups of activities, physics and engineering, and its main interest was the establishment of standards—scientific refinements, as it were, on the standard yard and the standard pound. But its interests soon widened; in 1910 it had branched out into metallurgy, aerodynamics and ship hydrodynamics. The full awakening to the significance of what science might be able to do—although perhaps not to exactly what kind of thinking it was—came with World War I. It is astonishing to recall that when the war began in 1914, although motor transport was then a feasible possibility and Henry Ford was in the process of setting up his moving assembly line, and although telegraphs and telephones were quite commonly in use, almost the only sign in the British Army of sixty years of applied science (using the word in its modern sense) were the sixty-three aeroplanes of the Royal Flying Corps. On the outbreak of war the British Army had a total stock of eighty motor vehicles. Guns and supplies were drawn by horses; each infantry division had 5,600 horses to its 18,000 men. Messages were carried from one unit to another, or to and from headquarters, by officers on horseback just as they had been in the time of Napoleon a century before. There were in 1914 no field telephones or wireless.

The war soon changed this attitude to science. Telephones and radio were introduced. The use of chemical gases—chlorine, phosgene and then mustard gas—was found to be feasible and was introduced, even though the social conscience pricked a little. Zeppelins, ineffective monuments of applied science and technology, bombed London. This was at first thought by the British to be particularly wicked, but conscience did not restrain them from retaliating on the civilian population of Germany when suitable aircraft were available. It became apparent that applied science was an activity that needed to be encouraged for the good of the nation. In 1917, the Department of Scientific and Industrial Research was set up to develop science as a community activity quite apart from the special efforts temporarily devoted to the war effort. And the National Physical Laboratory was absorbed into the D.S.I.R. as one of its constituent parts. In forty years' time it grew into an establishment employing 1,350 people run by a Director, a Deputy Director, a Secretary and nine Superintendents. The work then done at the N.P.L. ranged from biophysics to ship hydrodynamics. It drew its substantial finance from the Treasury on the basis of a 'rolling' five-year plan capable of some modification should new ideas suggest that such changes might lead to new discovery. The whole great organisation was run by a Department of State, the Ministry of Technology. It employed men of the highest intellectual calibre and scientific ability.

By the middle of the twentieth century, that is by the end of the period about which I am writing, it was implicitly assumed that anything that a nation wished to do could be done provided enough money was invested in the project and sufficient scientific thought applied to it. The Government, reflecting the popular belief, operated the D.S.I.R. to make discoveries by applying science to industrial problems. The Medical Research Council demonstrated the correctness of the thesis that new knowledge could be produced at will provided the will to produce it was sufficiently well financed and organised. M.R.C. workers won Nobel Prizes for discoveries of the first importance to medicine. No longer need people fear a new disease—poliomyelitis, let us say, or Asian influenza. The Government would find a way—by using science—to deal with the situation. Had not tuberculosis virtually ceased to exist as a major public-health hazard? What then could science not do?

The science-based nations of the world all desired to make faster and faster aircraft in the mid-twentieth century. Having accepted the thesis that scientific effort must be able to achieve anything, all that was needed to manufacture an aeroplane as fast as you please was to invest sufficient money and people in scientific research. In Great Britain, the Royal Aircraft Establishment was set up and soon employed 8,500 people. Many of these were test pilots and others engineers but at the centre was a core of scientists. They studied the behaviour of wings in wind-tunnels. Metallurgists investigated the performance of different alloys under stress. Chemists studied the performance of lubricants and fuels of different compositions. Dr M. J. Lighthill, the Director, was unashamedly in favour of bigness. For him, if the 8,500 people in the establishment made many useful discoveries, 17,000 people, if he could get them and the British Government were prepared to pay for them, would, he assumed, make even more numerous and doubly useful discoveries. 'There are almost no limits,' he wrote in 1962, 'to the benefits that size can confer,' and he claimed that whatever subject came up for investigation there would always in the Royal Aircraft Establishment be 'someone who knows all about it'.

The event of all others that led advanced communities finally to see that the scientific way of thinking with its application to practical problems was something to which the State ought to dedicate itself was the explosion of the atomic bomb over Hiroshima in 1945. This immense force so dramatically deployed—a populous city converted into a ruin in the twinkling of an eye—demonstrated beyond all cavil that the study of so esoteric a topic as nuclear physics could be of practical significance. In the United States, France, Russia, the Scandinavian countries and elsewhere national institutes were set up to study nuclear physics, that is, the composition and structure of the ultimate core of matter. In Great Britain, the U.K. Atomic Energy Authority was built up. In its prime, with Calder Hall and Chapelcross, making plutonium for bombs and carrying out research on chemistry and physics and the nature of isotopes, it soon came to employ 6,000 people. And only the best brains, scientists with the highest qualifications and the most brilliant talents, were employed.

It is interesting to note that as the 1950s gave place to the 1960s, the strictly utilitarian objectives of the Atomic Energy Authority changed. Although bombs and power stations remained the principal justification for the expenditure of very large sums of the nation's money, large additional amounts of treasure and substantial numbers of the most highly gifted men in the community were dedicated to researches in physics, not aimed at any particular material goal, but as an act of national faith. In earlier centuries, religious faith was more strongly based than it is now on the hope of practical results. Men feared excommunication because of their belief that it condemned them to fire and brimstone and interminable distress in the next world. Equally, their devotions would insure such practical ends as victory in war, freedom from epidemic disease and rain for the crops. For these reasons, among others, they devoted a significant proportion of the common wealth to the building of towering cathedrals and the installation in them of ornaments of gold and silver and fine linen.

In the mid-twentieth century beside the capital invested in nuclear piles and the 6,000 scientists researching at Harwell, the British nation also set up near by the Culham Laboratory, a fantastic structure as big as Buckingham Palace containing lecture rooms, offices, a library and great machines for concentrating 'plasma', as it is called. In preparations covering weeks, an experimental campaign would be organised so that, for one brief instant, a flash as bright as the sun—and I purposely choose these words—would be produced and perhaps nuclear fusion achieved. This operation was, in its way, as much an act of faith as in a different period of history was Moses holding out his arms over the battle so that the Children of Israel should prevail.

For nations to believe so strongly in the philosophy of science as to devote a major effort to the elucidation of truth is undoubtedly a matter of historical significance. In 1956, besides the establishments about which I have just written, there was set up in England the Rutherford High Energy Physics Laboratory. This was again a major installation housing big 'particle accelerators' for the study of physical phenomena only found to exist under very special conditions. To operate these machines a staff of 954 people was required. The purpose of this investment was to provide facilities for university scientists to carry out researches with equipment far too costly to be within their reach without the help of an enormously well-endowed patron. An historical parallel was the building of an elaborate astronomical observatory by King Frederick II of Denmark on the Island of Heven for Tycho Brahe in 1576.

An even more striking illustration of the belief of educated men of the mid-twentieth century in the virtues of science was the launching of CERN. The big wealthy nations—the United States, the Soviet Union, France, Great Britain and China—could afford to set up their own centres to study the new science of particle physics. Fourteen of the smaller nations of Europe—including Austria, Greece, Spain and Yugoslavia supported by major contributions from France,

Germany and Great Britain combined together to build and staff a large synchrocyclotron so that their scientists too could work on the frontiers of knowledge.

The mechanism of thought of which modern science consists has during the hundred years of 1850–1950 proved to be a potent means of achieving material results, and it is mainly for this reason that educated nations pursue new scientific knowledge. But science is also embraced for its own sake. The nations supporting the CERN establishment at Geneva may hope for cheaper nuclear power but their investment and co-operation are also an act of faith that some unforeseen good may emerge. In bringing this historical sketch towards its conclusion it is perhaps interesting to reflect on a curious side-issue bearing on the efficiency of science as a provider of material goods.

The British, American and Russian taxpayers who see millions of pounds of their money poured into Harwell and Culham and the domes and towers of secret places guarded by fences and gates have little idea of what is being done or what will emerge. But the peoples of Melanesia, the group of Negro-inhabited islands including New Guinea, Fiji, the Solomons and the New Hebrides lying between Australia and the open Pacific Ocean knew even less what science is about. And then, into their quite complex social organisation and elaborate religious belief and ritual—an organisation based, to be sure on technology using wood and stone rather than metal, but exhibiting highly developed culture as measured by the standards of maritime and agricultural ingenuity—came people of quite different culture: planters and traders from Great Britain, administrators from Australia or, at one time or another, organised and highly technological armies of men from Japan and the United States. The Melanesians observed these men carefully and saw that although they were wealthy and possessed canned food and wrist watches, radio sets, soap, outboard motors and clothing, cigarettes, whisky and bicycles beyond—one would imagine—the dreams of avarice, yet they did no work. To be sure, they wrote on pieces of paper or spoke into machines which were connected to radio antennae; having done so, cargo arrived in ships or aeroplanes.

Besides watching what these men did the Melanesians listened to what their missionaries said about Christianity, that in due time a Saviour would come and bring their heart's desire. They already believed that man's activities—whether gardening, sailing canoes or bearing children—needed magical assistance. Ritual without human effort was not enough. But neither was human effort on its own. And so it happened that officials of the Australian Government journeying into the central highlands of New Guinea came upon devotees of the 'Cargo Cult'. The people proceeded to butcher all their pigs, destroy their secret ritual objects and, in exchange, set up mock wireless antennae of bamboo and rope to receive in advance the news of the millenium and—knowing nothing of factories and the complex industrial system upon which they are based—the believers sat dressed in European clothes round tables with bottles of flowers in front of them waiting for the cargo ship or aeroplane to materialise. Others prepared magic pieces of paper and inscribed cabalistic writing on them.

Numerous instances of this curious mystical belief in science have been recorded. The first, the Milne Bay Movement, was as long ago as 1893 in Massim, New Guinea; the most recent, the Ninigo Islands Movement in 1945 and the Paliau Movement in the Admiralty Islands in 1946. The bizarre forms which some of the different manifestations of the Cargo Cult have taken must not blind us to the parallelism which they bear to the status which science has assumed in some sections of Western society. The most obvious result of the adoption of a scientific philosophy during the past century has been the increase in the industrial productivity of each individual man.

Technological nations in which this historical development has taken place know where the bicycles and whisky, the computers, motor-cars and electricity power stations, which support the 'gross natural product', come from. Although such communities do not sit waiting like Melanesians for a shipload of 'Cargo' to materialise, yet their aim is not entirely clear. Governments, by which the community purpose is expressed, have a good deal of day-to-day business to transact. The wars, Napoleon's at the start of the science century, the war of 1870, World War I of 1914, World War II of 1939, the technologies of which we have briefly discussed, the Korean War of 1953, the Vietnam War of 1964, have not solved the problems of which they were symptoms. Perhaps, however, the new scientific developments of nuclear weapons capable of destructive force sufficient to exterminate every human creature many times over—technically described as 'overkill'—and rockets capable of reaching any target no matter how distant, may lead at last to an alternative to military force for solving political problems.

Besides war, governments also have certain internal problems of administration, the transport of food and goods, the provision of water, fuel, medical and public health services, greater or lesser responsibilities for housing. All these tend to keep Officers of State busy. The very success and efficiency of applied science as a social tool has, however, tended to blind administrators to the fact that, whatever science itself may be, technology is a means to an end, not an end in itself.

At the beginning of the period of history which we are discussing, that is in the middle of the nineteenth century, although there were nations which could legitimately have been described as rich—Great Britain, perhaps, was one of these—there were many poor people in them. One need only read about Dickens' England of Oliver Twist or Tolstoy writing of a Russia of serfs to appreciate this without studying records of wage-rates or statistics of Poor-Law relief. But in the 'developed' countries—the United States, Great Britain, Scandinavia, France—a hundred years later, the total wealth of the community was great and the social organisation by which wealth was distributed was vastly more efficient and complete. Yet even so the belief in greater and greater investment in science, the construction of more roads occupying significant proportions of the available agricultural land, cutting directly through the hearts of cities, the parallel dedication of territory for airfields also infringing on the beauty, quiet and attractiveness of the places they were designed to serve, the continuous unrelenting pursuit of an ever-rising 'standard of living'—all these signs of faith in science as a bringer of social happiness unquestionably bore some relationship to the Melanesian Cargo Cults.

Clearly, when philosophers of particularly well-endowed nations such as, for example, the United States or Sweden, considered the matter, the application of scientific thinking primarily to material objects could be seen no more to insure social happiness than the faith of Pacific Islanders in the arrival of a ship-load of fairy bicycles. Science, however, has pervaded other areas of human activity than those concerned with economic wealth, physical health and military power. It has during the course of the century been directed to the study of the behaviour of man himself.

Professor Eysenck pointed out in 1960 that science has compelled

161

men to reconsider their own status in three important respects. First of all, in 1543 Copernicus, the Polish astronomer Nicolaus Koppernigk, with his book *De revolutionibus orbium coelestium*, displaced the earth from the centre of the universe of sun, moon, planets and stars and reduced it to the status of an insignificant satellite. Next, in 1850 Darwin showed that far from ranking as a unique being superior to all brute creation man was in fact first cousin to an ape. Third and last, Pavlov the great Russian physiologist showed in work extending over the first three decades of the twentieth century that much of human activity and behaviour can be accounted for, as can the behaviour of animals, in terms of simple associations of a purely chance nature between stimuli—pain, noise, bright light, smell and the like—impinging on man's sensory surfaces, his skin, ears, eyes or nose and the responses of his glandular or nervous systems. What Pavlov showed was that very many of the human responses which people assume to be due either to a mythical 'human nature' or—and this is hardest on non-scientific self-respect and arrogance—to what is assumed to be rational thinking and logical decision are simply due to the way we are 'brought up'. The scientific evidence marshalled by Pavlov clearly showed that many likes and dislikes, ideas about 'right' and 'wrong', views about marriage, the death penalty, the sanctity of the gold standard, patriotism, Sunday observance and the use of horse-meat for food have nothing whatever to do with human reason but are induced by a process of 'conditioning', the mechanism of which has been quite fully investigated.

Although the importance of Pavlov's discoveries was recognised in the first decade of the twentieth century and he was awarded a Nobel Prize in 1905, the implications of his work only gradually gained acceptance and, where they were applied to practical affairs, the decision to use them was taken as part of the general tide of ideas rather than being a conscious decision. But the tide of ideas brought a radical revolution in men's appreciation of some aspects of human behaviour as drastic as anything that occurred in the revolution of the science century. I refer to the reversal in people's views about madness.

Though Shakespeare, speaking for humane and intelligent men in the sixteenth century, wrote of madness as nothing more than being mad, the prevailing idea of the nature of insanity in Europe during the Middle Ages and beyond was that of demoniacal possession. The insane were not sick, but possessed of devils. To deal with insanity, to destroy the evil spirit accepted as gospel in pre-scientific times, torture and the cruellest form of treatment were employed. The insane were regarded with abhorrence and fear and were chained and relegated to cellars and dungeons. Even as late as the mid-eighteenth century when scientific ideas of observation and logical thought were beginning to spread and steam engines were being built, mildly insane people were cared for in shrines or allowed to wander about the country while those thought to be dangerous were locked up in ordinary prisons or chained up as they had been for centuries. The first person of the 'enlightened' eighteenth century to consider the facts of what had been for so long done and to appreciate the cruelty and horrible injustice of accepting dogma blindly was a French chemist and physician, Philippe Pinel. He published a book of 'medico-philosophical' studies of mental defectives in 1791 and in 1792, when he was made head doctor of two asylums, he released the lunatics from their chains and called for a more humane and thoughtful treatment of such unfortunate creatures. Not until 1838, however, were Pinel's arguments accepted at all widely even in France, and elsewhere in Europe and in the British Isles, the same old barbarous behaviour went on until the middle of the nineteenth century.

Gradually as the century progressed the principles of science—of observation, logical thought and experimental verification—were applied to the human mind as they were being applied to the human body by physiologists, biochemists and epidemiologists, using the discoveries of Pasteur and his successors as their scientific foundations. Finally, it began to be accepted that disordered states of mind, which in pre-scientific ages would have been attributed to maniacal possession, were to be recognised as being due to sickness. And in some instances the ways to cure the sickness were found. These could be drugs or the use of electric shocks or of surgery of the actual structure of the brain substance. This change in outlook, based as it was on knowledge, inevitably caused a philosophical change in moral outlook. What had been considered before to be crime, could also sometimes be seen to be sickness. And since the line between sickness and health is a blurred one, the pre-scientific certainty between 'right' and 'wrong' was also blurred.

The experimental observations of Pavlov and his successors showed that many of the 'ethical' beliefs of different societies did not necessarily possess any absolute validity but were simply the result of different conditioning in early life. A society must have its rules, but the philosophy of science, which insists that such matters must be examined and questioned and reviewed in the light of the facts as far as they can be determined, gives different answers from those derived from pre-scientific dogma. A curious example of the result of scientific challenge applied to the field of thought was Francis Galton's *Statistical inquiries into the efficacy of prayer*.

Galton, Charles Darwin's cousin, was a remarkable symbol of the challenge which scientific thinking must make to the outlook of the men who accept its validity. His first scientific work was a book, *Meteorographica*, published in 1863, a serious attempt to study weather. But soon he turned to the study of man. In 1869, he published *Hereditary Genius* in which he showed that statistical methods could usefully be applied to human talents. This led him to the study of finger-prints. He also carried out the first scientific investigations of instinct, mental imagery and, hence, of criminality.

The use of scientific thinking to study the nature of human behaviour and the human mind was inevitable. The essence of science is to challenge accepted tradition and to doubt accepted dogma. Copernicus and Galileo upset accepted ideas about the universe. Galton writing in the *Fortnightly Review* pointed out that 'the efficiency of prayer seems to me a simple, as it is a perfectly appropriate and legitimate subject of scientific enquiry'. And he then went on to marshal statistical evidence to show that prayer appeared to exert no measurable influence on the health of the Royal Family or on the weather. The average age attained by 97 members of Royal houses, who are extensively prayed for was, according to his table, 64·04 years, compared with 68·74 years for 513 people in trade and commerce who are hardly prayed for at all.

Although Galton's figures of 1872 may not stand scrutiny in the light of later scholarship, his philosophical approach epitomises the change of ideas brought about by the science century. Because behaviour once considered criminal may be found to be due to disease and outside the moral control of the individual perpetrating the act, this does not mean, however, that scientific discovery does away with right and wrong. As Galton put it, those whose approach to the universe is now based on scientific thinking 'know that they are descended from an endless past, that they have a brotherhood with all that is, and have each his own share of responsibility in the parentage of an endless future'.

It is interesting to trace the movement of opinion about the nature of science and its impact on behaviour from 1850, when its major implication with daily affairs really began, and a hundred or so years later. In the mid-nineteenth century adherence to rigid religious dogma had already been shaken. Gibbon in the *Decline and Fall of the Roman Empire*, written in the eighteenth century, had expressed serious doubts as to whether the rise of the Christian religion in Roman times had really been to the advancement of happiness and virtue in mankind. But at the time he wrote he found it necessary to express his views in guarded tones to avoid the charge of blasphemy. In 1832, however, University College, London—the so-called 'Godless College'—was set up to study the new knowledge of natural science in direct defiance of the two established English Universities of Oxford and Cambridge which would only accept students who publicly adhered to the Church of England. Yet Galton, writing forty years later but still in the same idiom, although insisting on his right to follow the truth wherever he believed it to lie and while unable to embrace the accepted dogma, could nevertheless express himself reverently thus:

> A confident sense of communion with God must necessarily rejoice and strengthen the heart, and divert it from petty cares, and it is equally certain that similar benefits are not excluded from those who on conscientious grounds are sceptical as to the reality of a power of communion. . . . The effort to familiarise the imagination with [the wonders of the universe as seen by scientific investigation] has much in common with the effort of communing with a God, and its reaction on the mind of the thinker is in many important respects the same.*

It is fair to say that at the beginning of the science century, while the population in general held to a devout respect for the tenets of religion, the men of science viewed the new knowledge they were uncovering with an equal feeling of reverence. As the century progressed, however, and applied science pervaded every aspect of social life more and more completely, the motives of action for so-called 'advanced' communities became more and more secular. The target of the twentieth century became the 'standard of living' rather than the good life. Aldous Huxley's bitter satire, *Brave New World*,

* *Fortnightly Review*, **68**, 125, 1872.

published in 1925, stood as a warning of too unthinking an acceptance of science for the material things it could do rather than for its illumination of truth.

But as the second half of the twentieth century followed the first and the second century of applied science began, it became apparent that the use of scientific thought in the affairs of life included something more than an ability to make nylon, antibiotics and nuclear piles. It could be seen that the changes brought about by science had come from action based on reason, evidence, imagination and doubt. These changes had included industrial wealth, increased amounts of food, the conquest of pain and disease, and understanding, both of Nature and of the nature and mind of man. It is because of the possibilities of using this understanding in an environment more completely under human control than has ever existed before, that the story of the century still to come will be even more remarkable than anything that has happened even in the hundred years of which this book gives a brief account.

The century that is passing has been a hundred years of revolution. This revolution has not been of one group of people against another but of an idea—the peculiarly powerful way of thinking we have called science—against other ways of handling the human situation. But now the revolution has happened and is in a fair way to be finished—just as the French Revolution is finished—what next? The Aswan High Dam is built, the Nubians can never go back. Nor can we. Consider what has happened. Labour-saving methods and machines and the application of computers to industrial productivity are already so far advanced that the curse of Adam—'by the sweat of thy face shalt thou eat bread'—is lifted. The man of the next century will relish work as a peculiar treat reserved for specially selected 'holy'-days. In another century, communication will be complete; no one need be out of sight or earshot of anyone else on earth; no one need wait for faster transport. A century ago, the horse could do its best, but as our transition age goes by, the fastest is the fastest: at 17,000 m.p.h. the vehicle is in orbit. Nourishing food, efficiently processed and tolerably well distributed to the cities where the human populations live, leaves stories of famine as memories of the past. Chemotherapeutic substances, antibiotics, vaccines and serums have already brought the main types of infectious disease under control and, together with reparative surgery and the subtle complexities of biological engineering providing mechanical kidneys, hearts, bones, joints and muscles, make many of the old pestilences of mankind little more than historical anachronism. Already it is recognised that the human population possesses the knowledge and power to control its own numbers.

In this book I have attempted to sketch the short historical period —the science century—lying between the long, rich story of the pre-scientific growth of civilisation and what may be a longer, richer period of man's maturity, which lies ahead of the human race when the science century is behind it and mankind is learning to live with the material wealth and power and such intellectual illumination as science may have given.

INDEX

Abel, Sir Frederick A. (1826–1902), and guncotton, 38
Acts of Parliament,
Diseases Prevention (1948), 26
Factory (1933), 113
Nuisances Removal (1848), 26
Post Office (1657), 84
Public Health (1848), 26
Aerial Experiment Association, Bell and, 97
aerodynamics, early ignorance of, 66
Africa, effect of scientific methods on its ecology, 147–9; plague of hippopotamuses, 148; groundnut disaster, 148; the Aswan High Dam, 149
aeronautics, and the speed of travel, 13, 14, 156–7
agriculture, effect of scientific thinking on, 9, 117; use of artificial fertilisers, 113, 132–3; application of chemistry to, 132–3, 137; history of increased wheat production, 132–6; use of machinery appliances, 140–2
airships, 66, 155
Albert, Prince Consort (1819–61), death from typhoid fever, 17–18, 19, 96; Presidential Address to British Association, 63, 107; and the Great Exhibition, 154
Alcock, Sir John (1892–1919) and Brown, Sir Arthur Whitten (1886–1948); fly the Atlantic, 67
America, use of scientific knowledge, 8; population increase in, 9, 142; use of nitre-beds, 38; explodes the atomic bomb, 49–50; growth of railways, 57–8; development of the motor-car, 62, 67; urbanisation of its population, 116; rust-resisting wheat production, 134; introduction of agricultural machinery, 140, 141, 142; its industrialisation, 142; high density areas, 144; and nuclear physics, 157

anaesthetics, discovery of, 28–9, 104
ancient world, means of communication, 84, 86, 87; and the art of rhetoric, 86; attitude to practical arts, 86, 101; knowledge of chemistry, 104; use of cement, 123; famines in, 145
animal husbandry, scientific improvements in, 136–8
antibiotics, discovery of penicillin, 30; other agents, 31
antiseptics, Lister and the control of bacterial infection, 29
Archimedes (c. 287–212 B.C.), 7, 45, 101
Argand, Aimé (1735–1803), his lamp, 71
Aristotle (384–322 B.C.), 4
armaments, technological advances in, 35 ff., 44, 49; breech-loading introduced, 37; discovery of guncotton, 38, 39; preparation of nitroglycerine, 38, 39; discovery of dynamite, 38, 39; use of 'aromatic' nitro compounds, 39; invention of percussion cap, 39–40; use of in naval warfare, 41–3; universal improvement in, 44; become of limitless destructive power, 50; their state in World War I, 155
Aspdin, Joseph and William, and Portland cement, 124
astronomy, 27; use of radar in, 48
Aswan High Dam, sacrifices the Nubians, 149, 166
atomic bomb, explosion of, 49–50, 157
Atomic Energy Authority, its objectives, 157
Austen, Jane (1775–1817), and the contemporary social scene, 6, 7
Australia, scientific history of wheat-growing, 135–6; its industrialisation, 142
automation, 126; basis of, 152

179

Wright, Wilbur (1867–1912), and Orville (1871–1948), airplane pioneers, 67

X-rays, discovery of, 40

Yeager, Charles, exceeds speed of sound, 67

Zeppelin, Count Ferdinand von (1838–1917), 66

Zurich Polytechnic, founding of, 154